This is a book of pleasure

Touch is the oldest and truest form of
communion. Work through this book
with a lover or friend. It's going to
teach you a new way of touching and
being touched.

Touch and massage are an expression of sensuality. No special knack is needed. No great knowledge of anatomy or strange techniques. With only a warm, quiet place and a bottle of scented oil you can spread pleasure inch by inch, soothe away care, and imbue tranquillity.

Sensitivity of touch can lend warmth to a new relationship or bring fresh life to a flagging one. It can bring intimacy to sex and sensuality to love.

The Art of Sensual Massage is written with a pleasant blend of friendliness and humour and warmth. Like massage it is something to enjoy at leisure, a book to browse through. It includes over 200 photographs and hints on oils and scents and erotic massage.

'Beautifully produced: a book to give, especially if you'd like its techniques used on you.'

Cosmopolitan

'Attractive as well as instructive . . . tells you what to massage, when and where. Much recommended.'

Forum

'If you want to encourage the man in your life to be more sensual, romantic and inventive . . . put *The Art of Sensual Massage* in his stocking.'

Miss London

the art of sensual
MASSAGE

by Gordon Inkeles & Murray Todris
with photographs by Robert Foothorap

London
UNWIN PAPERBACKS
Boston   Sydney

First published in Great Britain by George Allen & Unwin
1973
Reprinted twice
First published in Unwin Paperbacks 1977
Re-issued 1979

Reprinted 1979 and 1980

UNWIN® PAPERBACKS
40 Museum Street, London WC1A 1LU

British Library Cataloguing in Publication Data

Inkeles, Gordon
   The art of sensual massage.
   1. Massage
   I. Title   II. Todris, Murray   III. Foothorap,
   Robert
   613.7'9   RA780.5

   ISBN 0-04-613036-5

This book was originally published in the USA and American
spelling and usage have been retained.

Printed and bound in Great Britain
by Hazell Watson & Viney Ltd, Aylesbury, Bucks

To Matthew Inkeles, 1900–1961

There is but one temple in the Universe, says the devout Novalis, and that is the human body. Nothing is holier than that high form. We touch heaven when we lay our hand on the human body.—*Thomas Carlyle, The Hero As Divinity.*

the art of sensual
MASSAGE

The idea for a book on Sensual Massage originated a little over a year ago. I was living in Berkeley, doing some writing and building a massage practice in the East Bay. Everyone I worked with wanted to learn massage and, as a result, I organized what I hoped would be a series of small intimate workshops. When better than two hundred people responded to a few ads, I decided to put together a book of massage—something everyone could take home and use.

It has been a hard year with a few good turns that helped make this book and put it in your hands today.

I am greatly indebted to Murray Todris, the owner of the Normandy Massage Studios. Murray has had thirty-five years experience in this profession. Without his good will, technical assistance, and financial aid this book would never have appeared.

I wanted the book to be a technical manual, a tool, that was beautiful the way massage is beautiful. Four successive photographers tried to capture the sensuality that is part of every massage. But ultimately it was Robert Foothorap who proved I wasn't dreaming. If genius is accomplishment, then you must look closely at Foothorap's work. He is, first of all, a perfectionist. The pictures that illustrate the text were chosen from better than three thousand negatives. He printed every photograph himself. Working with a series of tight deadlines Foothorap completed this entire effort, three thousand photographs and hundreds of prints, in just under three months!

God, or somebody, bless Barbara Kelman, the Straight Arrow editor who took the text home and massaged her fiancé—the best reading I could have hoped for. And I want to thank Jon Goodchild. His clear head and gentle spirit produced a beautiful jacket and book design.

Finally, special thanks to all the people who let us use their homes for photography, and to Officer R. of the California Highway Patrol who said, 'I got nothing against it myself, just don't smoke that stuff on the bridge.' ❧

Gordon Inkeles
P.O. Box 583, Half Moon Bay,
California 94019

January 1972

Contents

3 _An Extended Massage_

4 _Appendix_

Wherefore I put thee in rememberance
that thee stir the gift of God, which is
in thee by putting on of my hands.—
Timothy II, Chapter 1, verse 6.

Preparation

1.

{Introductory Remarks}

There are no special tricks to massage—no hours of practicing weird techniques—no tedious new vocabulary to learn. With a warm quiet place and a bottle of scented oil you can spread pleasure over every inch of your partner's body. You don't need a lot of money or a room full of special equipment to do this. People were massaging each other before money or special equipment existed. And you don't need an intensive course in anatomy to lay your hands on another human being. The art of sensual massage is much older than any labels moderns have invented for the body.

Massage, like music, is what Aldous Huxley called a "psycho-physical skill." "... did Bach know how his muscles worked? No. But he played the organ very well and was a magnificent teacher. If proficiency in any psycho-physical skill depended on correct knowledge of physiology there would have been no good singers, dancers, pianists, runners and so forth until the middle of the twentieth century."[1]

After 400 years of Puritan oppression, Americans are painfully cold people. Since nearly all physical contact is construed as potentially sexual, people constantly avoid touching each other. Those "licensed" to touch, like Doctors, Barbers, Hairdressers, and Tailors, are careful to remain as impersonal as possible lest they be accused of making an advance. The simple fact remains, however, that you can use your hands to bring immense pleasure to another human being without the coldness of traditional therapy and outside the intimacies of sex. There is a wide spectrum of human feeling between the poles of therapy and sex—we call it the sensual. Once you get past the absurd taboos that inhibit sensual expression in our society, you can use massage to bring pleasure to a great many people.

You don't have to be sexually involved with everyone you touch. You can massage your friends, your parents, and your new aquaintances. "But," argues the Puritan, "certainly if you're rubbing somebody's legs you're making a sexual advance." Perhaps we should point out that by certain Arabic standards an unveiled woman's face is outrageously brazen and shamefully immoral.

[1] Laura Archera Huxley. *This Timeless Moment.* Ballantine Books, New York: 1968. p. 53.

These strokes that spread such satisfaction and pleasure can be marvelously therapeutic. Throughout history massage has been used to relieve suffering. The most ancient medical records speak of it routinely as though it were one of the physicians most valuable tools. Massage was used to promote healing long before the deluge of modern drugs which have supposedly freed doctors from laying a hand on a patient. We will discuss therapeutic applications of various movements occasionally. But when you yourself work with these strokes you'll discover their healing power.

Pleasure and therapy—depends on what you want to do.

In a world full of expensive gadgets futilely designed to increase enjoyment of life it is enormously satisfying to realize that you can give so much pleasure just using your hands. Massage can be an exquisitely sensual experience, beyond description or imagination.

{Oils & Essences}

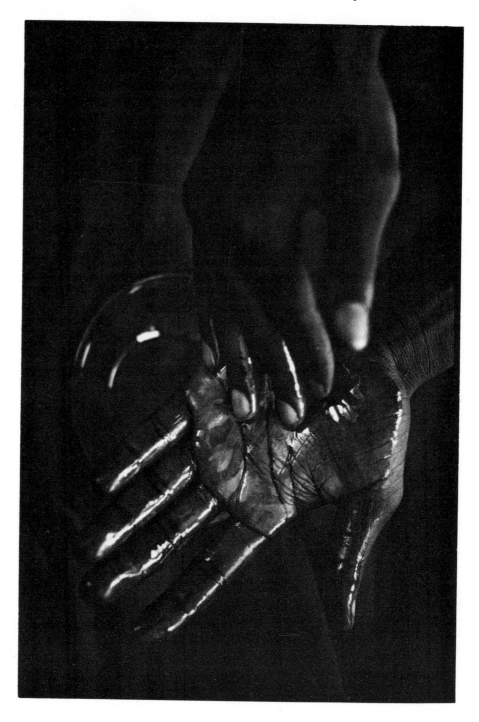

The Biblical word anoint very often means to massage with oil. The ancient Jews used olive and vegetable oils to warm the skin of those they wished to bless. In the past five thousand years no better massage oils have been discovered.

Any vegetable oil, with the exception of peanut or corn oil, makes a fine base. Coconut oil is exceptionally clean and colorless. When it is heated it liquifies into a smooth almost odorless medium. Safflower oil is less expensive and easier to use because it doesn't solidify at lower temperatures. Keep your oil in a bottle or metal bowl that isn't likely to tip over while you're working. Use a coffee warmer or candle to heat the bowl so that you have warm oil throughout the massage. Cold oil on warm skin will shock your partner and break the mood.

Once your oil is warm, scent it with an essence extract, a perfume, or a few drops of fresh lemon juice. Odor determines mood as surely as lighting, music, and touch. So pick your scent carefully. It's a good idea to have a few bottles on hand for your partner to choose from.

Oil each part of the body before you begin massaging it. Oiling is a delicious feeling—let your partner relish it. Pour the oil onto your hands then spread it slowly with even circular strokes. You need just enough oil so that your hands will move smoothly. Too much oil will leave your partner dripping. Hairy parts of the body take a bit more oil than smooth skin. Go easy on the head and hands.

Oil comes off with a soft towel. Wipe it off gently before your partner turns over, after you finish the feet, and once again after completing the massage. Rubbing down the skin with alcohol is an even more effective way of removing oil. Alcohol has to be used cold though and cold alcohol is a jolt. Some people love it and won't do without an alcohol rubdown during a massage. More commonly, though, the shock destroys the mellow vibrations you've worked to maintain.

{ *Preparation for Massage* }

*L*ock the door and take the phone off the hook. Touch your partner while you read this. Anywhere.

Massage aims to relax all the senses. Your preparation should center on this idea.

Light. Nobody keeps his eyes open through a massage. Make it easy for your partner to drift away from visual distractions. Lighting should be soft and indirect. A well shaded lamp is fine. Candlelight or an oil lamp is even better. Or work in the dark some night when the moon is up.

Quiet. If you're indoors listen to the room. Every room has its own sounds and they become very apparent while you're stroking. If the two of you like the message you may want to let it go on. Otherwise music is a wonderful way to fill a massage room. Something easy and smooth. Flutes, Classical Guitar, Slow Blues, a Raga or Chant. Of course if you're outdoors it's all there waiting for you.

Warm. At least 75 degrees. Your partner barely moves while you're stroking and will feel even the slightest chill in the room long before you do. Be sure your hands are warm before you begin touching.

Taste. You know what he likes.

The body. Most people like a hot bath or shower before massage. A sauna is fine too if you have one. If you do use a sauna, wait at least twenty minutes after the final bath for the body to cool thoroughly before you begin massage. Whatever you decide on be sure both of you are clean. Trim your fingernails. Stay off waterbeds and soft mattresses if you're serious about massage. Your partner needs to rest on a fairly level surface. It's easy to create one on a warm beach or a grassy field with perhaps a heavy blanket and sheet to smooth over bumps, grit, and dust. Indoors, look for a thick rug or a few large flat pillows like the ones you see in this book.

You can cover your pillows with sheets or, for a few dollars more, with velvet, silk, and satin fabrics the way we did.

You may want to give extra support with cushions under the small of the back, below the ankles, and behind the neck.

Incense. Sure—the long burning kind.

Be sure everything is where you want it before you begin so you can avoid short jerky motions and interruptions.

Repeat movements three times (unless otherwise noted). When your partner gets excited about something you're doing keep it up for awhile.

Be sure there are no serious skin, joint, or muscle problems before you begin massaging. Your partner should remove contact lenses before you begin. Work around bruises, cuts and abrasions. In any case, if anything you do causes pain, stop, and go on to another part of the massage. *Never hurt your partner.* Use pressures that feel good to him.

Touch and stroke as much as possible all through the massage. Use the full surface of your hands keeping your fingers together. All movements should blend into each other in a single smooth motion. Touch your partner when you move from one part of the body to another, making the contact seem continuous and a part of the massage.

Be silent.

The strokes that follow give you enough technique for a complete body massage. Use them to work on the whole body or any part of it. While you learn you may want to improvise a bit as you develop a personal massage style—but always remember to keep your stroking rhythmic, even and symmetrical. Don't worry too much if you don't get a stroke perfectly the first time through. All touch feels good.

One of the really fine things about massage is that it allows people to forget about clocks and schedules. The body alive outside of time. ❧

A Complete Body Massage

2.

{The Abdomen & Chest}

Peace

I am warm
  from your touch:
    flower/eye
    body/body
    creature/god
  We are all warm.

     Charles Paisley

Abdomen and Chest

Although you can start a massage any-where, the abdomen feels good because it's in the middle of the body. Most massage movements are symmetrical and by beginning at the middle of the body you can spread warmth and relax-ation evenly in all directions.

The tone of the stomach and the large and small intestines are particu-larly important in determining the mood of muscles and nerves throughout the body. A few minutes spent working around the digestive area as you begin will enhance the entire massage. Re-member that your first strokes here will establish the rhythm for the next hour or so. The great mistake in the early stages of massage is to shorten strokes and try to hurry on to what you believe to be more important parts of the body. If you feel tightness in the digestive area, work on it slowly and evenly per-haps for a few extra minutes. On the abdomen you will get satisfaction by in-creasing the number of movements, not the *pressure* of individual strokes. Re-member, work into a regular easy rhythm now at the beginning of the massage and stay with it. 🍃

Swimming

Swimming is one of the easiest massage movements to learn. It is used on all parts of the body but it feels particularly good across the broad muscles of the abdomen and chest.

Begin with your hands flat on either side of your partner's abdomen and slide them, pressing gently, to the opposite side. Repeat this movement three times and then, as you return on the final stroke of the third movement, move the hands up about three inches and begin again. This way the swimming movement will flow gradually up and down the abdomen and chest slowly covering the entire area. Stroke as high as the shoulders but be careful to stay off of the throat. When you reach the shoulders move down to the abdomen and then return to the shoulders once more.

If you're working on a woman, don't try to avoid the breasts. Stopping below the breasts and continuing above them, or somehow working around the breasts will only break the rhythm of the stroke and embarrass both of you. ❧

Stroking Beneath the Lower Ribs

Beginning at the center of the body use the three middle fingers to trace a line parallel to the lower ribs all the way to the side. Use moderate pressure as you press down below your partner's ribs. When you reach the side lift your hands and return to the starting position. This stroke is a bit unusual since you must lift your hands off the body while you're working. This lift though, and others like it on different parts of the body, need not interrupt the rhythm of massage. Use the lift the way a musician uses silences to enhance the dramatic effect of a composition. You can do this by developing a consistent timing for the lift; the hands leaving the body for the same amount of time each time they are lifted.

'Many have, no doubt heard of the invalid lady who was suffering from constipation and, as a result of this, indigestion. Her friend, calling one afternoon, inquired, "Do you ever knead your bowels?" The invalid lady meekly replied, "Indeed, ma'am, I cannot very well do without them." The resulting burst of laughter shook up the abdominal viscera to such an extent that the constipation was relieved, the indigestion was cured, and the patient got well.'[2]

[2]Douglas Graham, M.D. *Massage: Manual Treatments; Remedial Movements*. J. B. Lippincott Company. Philadelphia: 1913. p. 85.

Draining the Colon

The sides of the colon or large intestine are frequently caked with bits of half digested food and waste matter. Breaking up these crusty deposits aids digestion and, more important, helps to relax the smooth involuntary muscles throughout the entire intestinal cavity. Study carefully the sequence shown below. Raise your partner's knees for the duration of this stroke.

You're going to drain by pressing and stroking. The hands work in a circle following each other. Stroke with the palm of the left hand and press with the fingertips of the right hand.

The movement of the right hand follows a U shape course over the colon across your partner's abdomen. The left hand makes an uninterrupted circle. The repositioning of the right hand can be easily disguised by maintaining a smooth even motion with the left hand. The entire stroke should flow almost as a single motion. ❧

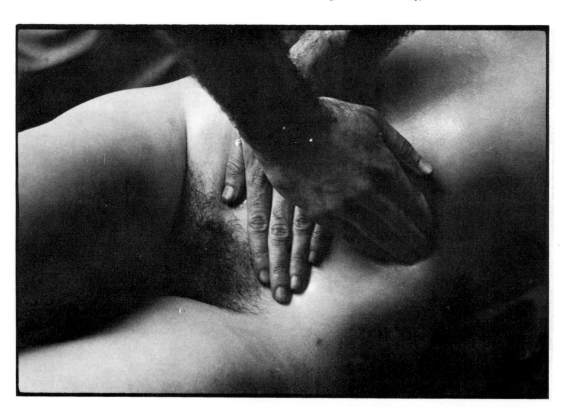

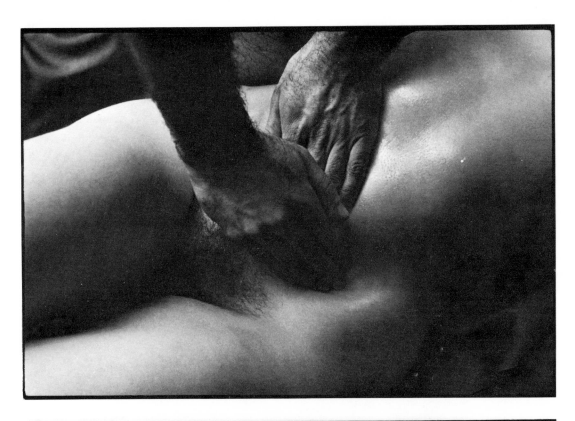

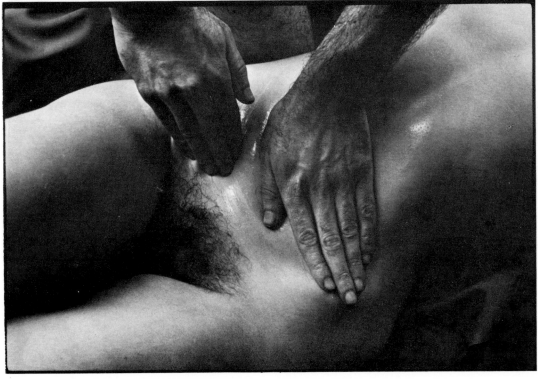

Fingertip Kneading the Waist

Strokes like this one have been used for a long time with people who want to take off a few pounds. But since kneading feels so good and aids the muscle tone of the abdominal area it is not merely therapeutic.

Pick up folds of flesh between the finger tips and the thumb across the waist and stomach. Knead with your fingertips as you would a piece of dough. The hands move in small circles, slowly, back and forth, lifting and turning, covering every inch of the abdominal area. Your partner will feel it if you skip even an inch or two. You can vary this stroke by gently shaking each fold of flesh before you begin kneading it. ❦

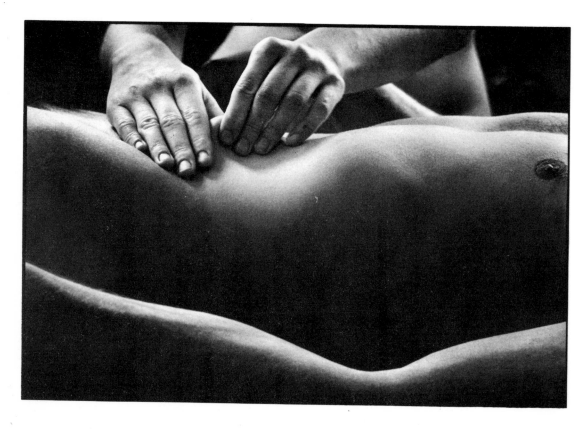

Kneading the Sides

Knead both sides of the chest with the full flat area of your palms and fingers. Rotate your hands in small circles as you move. Pick up the flesh between your hands. Feel it roll. Contact. You're working mostly with your fingers but all touch feels good. The touch of the palm. The feel of the heel of your hand gliding across the skin.

Begin just above the waist and work up the side to the armpit. Reverse the stroke at armpit and waist a half a dozen times. The kneading motion usually calls for grasping large folds of flesh. The chest, however, is not as meaty as the thigh and when working on slim people it's sometimes difficult to find a fold of flesh to lift. If that happens leave out the flesh lifting part of the movement. Don't grab at the flesh of the sides in an attempt to pinch some up between your hands. If it doesn't come easily then let it go. The kneading motion of the flat part of your hands will serve as a fine massage for a bony ribcage. ❧

Chest Circulation

Circulation strokes get the blood moving and warm the body. Be sure you've oiled the entire chest and abdomen before you get into this movement. The three photographs show you how this stroke looks.

Begin with your fingers pointing inwards and your palms flat. You're going to press upward across your partner's abdomen and chest. Just below the neck turn your hands out to the sides. Return to the original position pressing lightly against the sides. The pressure part of the circulation movement is the thrust up over the chest, not the return against the sides.

If you wish you can vary the circulation stroke by caressing the shoulders before you return along the sides. ❧

The Chest Lift

If you want to convert a woman to the pleasures of massage pay close attention to this stroke. Prepare for the chest lift by slowly rotating your cupped hands on your partner's shoulders. The front of the body should be well oiled by this time but it's usually a good idea to oil it a bit more before you begin. Gently lift the right shoulder and then the left and oil the back around and below the shoulder blades. After oiling return to simple rotation on the shoulder blades once again for fifteen seconds or so. The chest lift is described in the sequence of photographs.

Begin by pressing the flat of your hands, fingers pointed down, across the shoulders and down over the top of the chest. As you reach the breasts (or the chest of a man) turn the fingers of your

hands so that they face each other.

With your fingers lined up facing each other press the flat of your hands across the breasts and down to the waist. Turn your hands again at the waist so that your fingers rotate slowly onto the back, thumbs down. While you draw your hands up the back, *lift* about three inches. Your partner's back will rise snake-like from belly to breasts.

Return to the beginning of the stroke by turning your hands once on the shoulders. With a bit of practice the entire stroke will come off as a single motion even though you must turn your hands several times. The chest lift feels as good as it looks. For women massaging men the stroke works the same way but unless you've got a very strong back you'll need a massage table (see page 146) to bring it off smoothly. 🌿

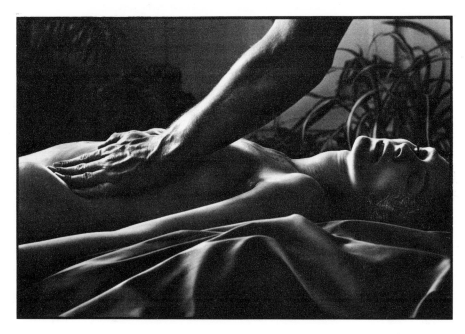

Deep Chest Massage

Full chested men appreciate a skillful deep chest massage. The strokes involved are amazingly simple considering the amount of pleasure they can give. Use the palm of your hand and the fingertips to work the thick, tough chest muscles. Begin with the two hands positioned crab-like on either side of the chest. Press the palms down and chisel the muscle ridges with your fingertips. Move down to the center of the abdomen releasing some of the pressure when you come off of the ribcage. Return, stroking gently. This massage works on women too but go very easy over the breasts. 🌿

{ *Neck & Head* }

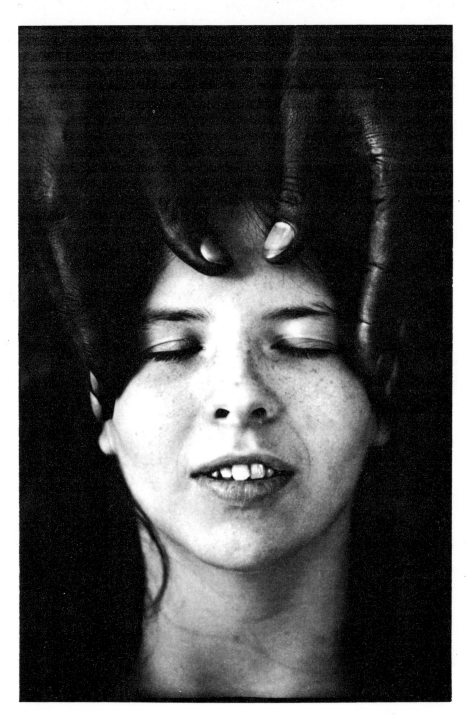

Turn off your mind,
relax and float downstream
   It is not dying. . . .
Lay down all thought,
surrender to the void
   It is shining
That you may see the meaning of with-
in
   It is feeling
     The Beatles.

We don't usually think of the head as a source of physical pleasure. To 'use your head' so often means merely to think, worry, and decide. But there is another, purely sensual way to use your head. Precisely because the head is one of the most sensitive parts of the body it can also be the source of the most gratifying and purely physical sensations.

Massage of the head is often neglected because this part of the body offers no large masses of muscle for the hands to manipulate. Neck and head strokes are not only possible, they are one of the most rewarding forms of massage. Frequently a violent headache can disappear in less than a minute if you know how to use your hands. In fifteen minutes of neck and head massage you can soothe the most jangled nerves. Women experience tension at the base of the neck more often than men simply because the head is quite heavy and it is tiring to carry it around.

Smooth those stubborn bundles of tight neck muscles and watch your partner's expression relax while you are working. This kind of massage not only relaxes and soothes the head, but is equally effective as a stimulus for mental activity. The mind is like a muscle. When you clear the nasal passages and stimulate the base of the brain, lightness and clarity take the place of heaviness and dullness. Relieve tension on the neck and spine at the point where they connect to the brain and the brain itself will relax.

Neck and Back Vibration

When performing this stroke upon your partner you may find it hard on your back if the two of you are on the floor. Try it once and see if your back can handle it. Slide both hands, palms up, fingers together, under the shoulders. Push down, oiling as you go, about six inches below the neck. Position your fingers on either side of the spine but stay off the spine itself. Press your fingertips up, lifting the back about two inches, and pull up along either side of the spine as far as the neck. Repeat this motion a half a dozen times and then jerk your fingers up and down as you pull up. This is the vibration effect. You'll use it again on other parts of the body where it comes off with a good bit less work. Get it working smoothly here and you'll have no difficulty with it later. Some people will try to help when you lift their back. Don't let them— remember that only you are putting forth any effort. Your partner should passively experience the sensuous effects of massage. ❧

Brain Rotation

Below the skull in the middle of the neck, the spinal cord merges with the lower part of the brain (the medulla oblongata). Every one of the thirty-one pairs of nerves that serve the body pass through this point. As you massage this area, remember that this is where sensation becomes thought. If you're working with long hair gently lift the head (remember *you* do the lifting) and stroke the hair back away from the neck. Do this by stroking several times up from the neck and along the skull. Hair stroking is a luxurious technique in itself. Remember never to move the hair around as if it were merely in the way. You can easily integrate hair movement with the massage by stroking and caressing it.

Press the first and second fingers of each hand into the depression under the center of the skull and rotate them slowly. Circle the top part of the center of the neck and push up gently under the skull. Your rotation should move in a pattern similar to the kneading motion on the neck—from vertical to horizontal. Quite often you will feel tension relaxing in thirty or forty seconds. But be careful not to offend the brain. Moderate pressure for a minute or a minute and a half will do. ❧

Pressing the Neck

The thick muscles at the back of the neck bear tension so often that many people hardly notice tightness in that area. Nevertheless, neck tension is very often the cause of immense physical and psychological fatigue. It's easy to sooth these muscles by lifting and stroking them.

With the fingers held together and the fingertips of each hand facing the other on the fleshy part of the neck press up on the back of the neck until you're lifting it slightly. Begin rotating your hands in tiny opposing vertical circles. One hand is up while the other is

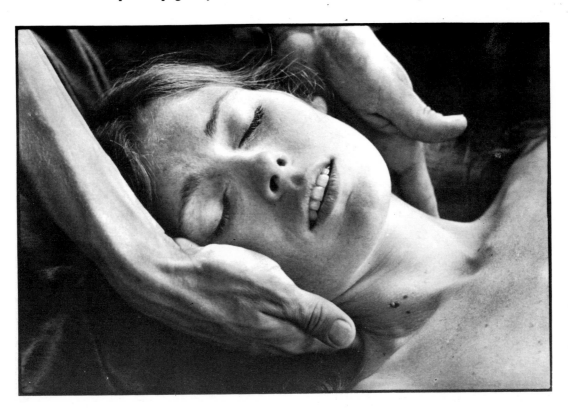

down; like a piston except the motion is circular. The flesh will rise and fall against your hands. You need not actually break contact with your partner's neck during this movement, but press up into the muscles at the top of each stroke. 🌺

Stroking Below the Ears

Just below the ears you can feel the lower edge of the skull curving back away from the jawbone. With the four fingers of each hand stroke the large band of neck muscles that meet the skull at this point. Move back and forth in a piston motion. Follow below the line of the jawbone. 🌺

Neck and Shoulder Stroking

Lift and slowly turn the head so that the right cheek is resting on the ground. Oil the side of the neck and below the shoulder. Use plenty of oil under the shoulder because you're going to have to fit your hand in there without lifting the chest. Cup your hand at the top of the neck as shown and slide it down the side of the neck and onto the shoulder. A number of large veins run through the side of the neck so you've got to go easy. The shoulder area takes the main force of this stroke. Feel it with your whole hand. Return, pressing up with your four fingers, the thumb gliding lightly along the neck. 🌺

Rotating the Head

We are always conscious of our heads as a physical presence. Whether we're walking, talking, or lying down, the head is a persistent weight that must be shouldered. The following strokes have the somewhat bizzare effect of 'detaching' the head from the rest of the body. Some rainy afternoon or evening take the time to extend them for fifteen or twenty minutes. Very stony.

With palms at the base of the skull lift the head very slowly until it is nearly upright. When you feel the neck muscles begin to tighten stop and position your hands for rotation. Turn the head very slowly and evenly. One revolution should take at least fifteen seconds. (On that rainy afternoon try two minutes for each revolution.) Make three complete revolutions to the right, pause ten seconds and make three revolutions to the left. Pause again at the upright position and press the head forward, gently, three times to stretch the neck muscles. Finish by lowering the head very very slowly to the ground. Grasp the head under the skull and under the chin and pull back moderately hard. Rotate twice in each direction (as above) while you pull. 🌱

Lifting and Pulling the Head

Hold your partner's head just under the chin and behind the skull (as in the photograph below) and lift it slowly just a few inches. Raised like this the head will rotate in a smooth arc from shoulder to shoulder. When you turn you will feel tension at both ends of the arc—be careful not to press beyond this point. With the head turned to one side, pull straight back on the chin moderately hard. While you are pulling begin to rotate slowly from one shoulder to the other. Move back and forth slowly and evenly five times. Hold an even pressure pulling back on the head while you turn. ✿

Third Eye Kinetics

Just as the lower brain is a neural center, the third eye is a kind of a focal point for head and face energies. Whether or not you believe the Buddhist doctrine that this spot is the seat of the soul you will find that it is an exquisitely sensitive energy center. Hold the fingertips of your right hand (palm down) a quarter of an inch in front of the third eye. Without even touching it you will feel its sensitivity. Because of the way it *feels* the third eye is the natural center for massage of the face. ❧

Temple Strokes

Iago—My Lord has fallen into an epilepsy; this is his second fit; he had one yesterday.
Cassio—Rub him about the temples.[3]

Center your temple strokes on the third eye. Press it lightly with each thumb while you rotate the first three fingers inside the slight depression that forms the temples. Some people like to rhythmically vary the pressure on the thumbs while they move the fingers. Try working the temples with a slow piston motion beginning at the top and ending at the corners of the eyes. As you move over the face return for a few of these soothing temple strokes from time to time. ❧

[3]William Shakespeare. *Othello*. Act IV, scene i, lines 51–53.
[4]Shakespeare, op. cit. Act III, scene iii, lines 284–288.

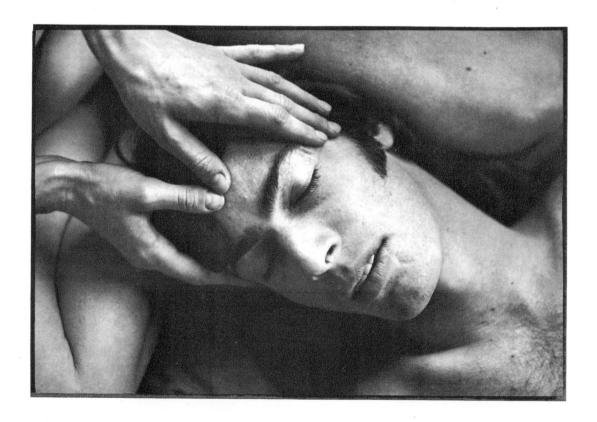

Forehead Press

Othello—I have a pain upon my forehead, here.
Desdemona—Let me but bind it hard, within the hour it will be well. [4]

The forehead press is simple and quite dramatic because it can very often be used to cure a nagging headache in a few seconds.

Press down with the entire left hand, palm, fingers and thumb. Use the right hand to add pressure and maintain an even force. You can exert a fair amount of pressure (your partner will tell you if it's too much) but reach maximum pressure very slowly. Then hold it for a silent count of ten seconds. Release gradually until just the center of the palm is touching the third eye. Then release this slight contact slowly. If you're working on a persistent headache combine this stroke with repetitions of neck kneading, brain rotation, and temple stroking.

The Eyes

Alain Bosquet—If you were condemned to perpetual incarceration within a totally dark cell, what would you do? *Salvador Dali*—I would create phosphenes. I would exert pressure on my eyes with my fingers to make an image emerge from my intra-retina. It's something I never have time for in my current life.[5]

There's no need to oil the eye. All you'll need is the bit of oil that's accumulated on your fingertips during the massage. Begin with the tip of your little finger on the inside corner of each eyelid. As you move that finger out,

pressing lightly on the eye and under the eyebrow, bring down the next finger into the place where the little finger began. One finger follows another in this pattern across the eye until you have all four fingers down touching each other, and moving very slowly. When the index finger reaches the outside corner of the eye gently press both thumbs onto the third eye. Repeat this exact process on the bottom ridge of the eye. Press lightly but rhythmically on the surface of each eyelid to show your partner what Dali is talking about.

End your eye sequence by returning to the temple strokes. 🌿

[5]Alain Bosquet. *Conversations with Dali.* E. P. Dutton and Company. New York: 1969. p. 62.

Turning the Cheeks—Opening the Mouth

With your hands flat, fingers pointed down on the cheeks (photo) rotate the flesh of the cheeks slowly but firmly. The lips will distort and roll as you turn the cheeks. Open the mouth by pressing down on the chin. The mouth will open easily if the head and neck are relaxed. If the mouth seems tense work on the neck a bit more and try again. If it's still tense let it go. When you encounter stubborn tension anywhere in the body do what you can and go on.

Remember that a single massage cannot always completely counteract the results of weeks or even months of tension. The first time through you'll break the ice and that alone is a great pleasure. Never chide your partner for being 'uptight,' nervous, or tense. That's the last thing they need. Tightness that stubbornly refuses to yield is involuntary. ❧

{ The Arms }

Holding hands, a simple expression of warmth so common in other parts of the world, is practically tabu in the United States. How many people do you know who hold hands with anyone outside of their immediate family?

Begin massage of the arms and hands by holding your partner's hand. Hold the forearm with your other hand. If you are massaging your lover, press your forehead (third eye) against the thick veins that run across the surface of the arm joint opposite the elbow while still holding arm and hand. This exquisitely tender act of worship allows the person under your hands to feel as though his body were a temple. It is.

Circulation

Since the arms carry the blood a long way from the heart your first concern here is blood circulation. The simple stroke for arm circulation is one of the basic massage movements. Variations of it will be used later for both sides of the legs and the back. Since most arteries run deep inside the body the circulation stroke primarily affects the venous network, the system that returns blood to the heart. The thrust of every circulation stroke is towards the heart. This movement not only aids the passage of blood, it stimulates the movement of lymph, and maintains and restores the tone of the muscles.

Oil the arms—hairy arms require more oil than smooth arms. Position your hands, (left hand on top for the right arm, right hand on top for the left arm) at the wrist. Stroke up the arm with even pressure, oiling as you go. When you reach the shoulder turn smoothly and return, pressing lightly with the flat of your palm and fingers against the sides of the arm. Lean forward on this stroke. Massage the arms with one long, sweeping, uninterrupted motion. The entire stroke is illustrated here in sequence. Repeat it ten times on each arm.

You will feel the long smooth muscles of the arm relax as you stroke them. ❧

Kneading the Arms

Although kneading focuses on a single small area as you work up and down the arm the effect is to warm up the entire arm. The results can be quite dramatic since the part of the arm you are kneading becomes almost weightless as you pass over it.

Lift the arm off of the ground by pressing your partner's hand against the side of your chest just below your armpit. Press in with your arm, as shown, and the arm will stay where you want it while you knead. Again, do not let your partner try to help—you lift the arm. The kneading motion is simple and enormously satisfying. Lift the underside of the arm with all four fingers of each hand and rotate the thumbs slowly in opposite directions over the muscular top of the arm. You'll feel the muscles of your partner's upper arm move under your thumbs. If it is a heavily muscled arm use plenty of pressure as you roll and press the muscles. With thin arms, particularly those of women and children, press more gently. Remember that if you press down hard on a bone you are probably hurting. Feel the *muscle*, not the bone, under your fingers. As you knead move down the arm slowly. When you reach the elbow, circle it three or four times with five fingers of each hand. Release the hand before you knead the forearm. With your partner's elbow on the ground knead slowly up the flat forearm to the wrist. Reverse the motion at the wrist and knead back up to the shoulder, circling the elbow and grasping the hand against your chest for upper arm kneading. Move up and down the arm like this four times. The arm relaxes as the muscles smooth out. ✣

Muscle Kneading

On thin or poorly muscled arms this stroke can be omitted. But you can manipulate the inside of heavily muscled arms exactly the way you knead the side of the chest (See page 20). Separations in arm muscles are deep and clearly defined. Feel into them as you work. ♣

Draining the Forearm

In this stroke you will be pressing the blood back through the venous system of the arm. This is done by holding the arm at the wrist and pressing with both thumbs down as far as the elbow. Vary the pressure, as you did when kneading, according to the thickness of the arm. Return to the wrist, lightly pressing the sides of the arm with the flat of your palm and fingers (See Circulation). ❧

Throwing

The next three strokes (Throwing, Snaking, and Rolling) create tensionless energy throughout the arm. Pick up the arm by the hand and elbow. Hold it straight up by the hand and toss it back and forth from one hand to the other. Begin with a small arc and gradually increase it. As you throw it you'll feel a sudden tightening; limit the arc at that point, or extend it so that the arm moves from a position nearly straight above the head to a point just over the knee. Throw the arm 4 times and at the end of the final pass catch it in a vertical position and hold it there for Snaking. ✤

Snaking

Hold the arm straight up by the hand and, beginning at the shoulder, press the flesh on both sides of the arm between the thumb and four fingers of the other hand. Slide this hand up the arm to the wrist pressing and releasing rapidly as you go. It's important to keep the arm vertical as you move. When you reach the wrist begin again at the shoulder pressing a bit to the right or left of your original path. Each time you begin this snaking motion, press a slightly different part of the arm. That way you will cover most of the muscles from more than a single angle. This compresses arm tissues which invigorates the muscles. Repeat the snaking ten times, varying the speed as you work from slow deliberate pressing to a very quick series of strokes up to the wrist. ✤

Rolling

Take this movement slowly at first. You'll need a bit of practice before you can run through it quickly. Begin by folding the arm at the elbow across the neck. Press the palms of each hand against either side of the arm just above the shoulder at the same spot where you began Snaking. Roll your hands back and forth in a piston motion pressing about as hard as you did when Snaking. As you roll begin to move up the arm slowly. When you reach the folded elbow continue to roll and press up. The arm will rise between your ascending hands. Roll up to the wrist and then fold the arm carefully and begin again. Repeat this stroke five times. Practice until the rolling and folding of the arm become as rhythmic as possible. Once you become sure of the movements you need for this tricky stroke the entire process will begin to flow despite the fact that you must break con-

tact with the arm several times. Like Snaking, Rolling invigorates the muscles. It's also a fine aid to circulation and will heighten the nutrition of the inner tissues of the arm. Feels good too.

Pulling And Turning The Arm

Lift the arm above the head and pull
it slightly so that there is no bend at
the elbow and a slight tension throughout the arm. Maintaining this tension
rotate the arm in a small arc above the
head three times in each direction.
From the same position pull the arm
gently. Pull out and then rotate again
once in each direction. These movements
excercise the complicated shoulder joint,
one of the most mobile parts of the
body. You can sometimes hear it turning as you rotate the arm. Heartbeat,
bone rumble, and skin whispers are all
part of the exotic natural music you and
your partner create, heard best when
massaging on a secluded hillside some
quiet summer afternoon. ❧

Brushing The Arms and Hands

Brushing is a good way to end arm
massage at the same time as you begin
working on the hand. Glide up and
down the arm and hand with your fingertips. Use both hands and let your
body sway back and forth rhythmically
as you move. Begin with short strokes
and end with long sweeping motions
that cover the entire arm. End with
just your fingertips touching your
partner's fingertips. Break this contact
very slowly. You may hear your
partner's almost imperceptible sigh as
your fingertips part. Listen.

{The Hands}

The hands, like the head, don't initially seem to offer much opportunity for massage. They are bony, thin, and relatively small. But the muscles and nerves of the hands are extremely active most of the day. We use our hands in whatever we do in life—they are the most mobile part of the body.

Hands are almost always the first part of the body to age. They wrinkle because there isn't enough natural lubrication available on the surface of the skin. Even the supposedly bare parts of the face like the forehead and cheeks, are actually covered with a fine network of hair follicles which work to restore natural oils to the skin. Oil keeps the skin supple and since hands are almost completely hairless the skin cracks easily. Using harsh soaps and detergents that totally dry out the skin greatly accelerates the process that eventually wrinkles the hands.

Sprinkle a few drops of lemon juice into your oil if the hands appear particularly dry. This simple measure helps to restore the skin's natural acidity. But whether you're trying to rejuvenate the skin or just simply relax the muscles remember that so much of what your partner feels is felt with hands and fingers. Hand strokes can be one of the most sensual parts of massage.

Hand Rotation

Begin massage of the hand by rotating it. Grasp your partner's hand around the lower part of the fingers with one hand and hold the arm steady with the other hand just below the wrist. Turn the hand so that it rotates in as wide a circle as possible. Don't force it, but press gently to the limits of the circle. Because of the structure of this part of the body, the hand will not turn in a perfect circle. As you turn you should feel it dip and bob. Rotate three times in each direction. Generally, most rotations will maintain this frequency. ❧

Kneading the Back of the Hand

Hold the palm of the hand with the
four fingers of each hand and rotate the
thumbs over the bony back of your
partner's hand exactly the same way
you kneaded the arm. Move in tiny circles over this entire area. You know
this stroke is working if you can *feel*
the bones as you massage them. 🌿

Rotating the Bones of the Hand

Massage is a gentle art. If you are a man *and* an expert masseur women may wonder about you. 'Is he actually capable of being that gentle? Can he really give me so much pleasure using just his hands?' One of these days, after you've put aside this book for awhile, you'll mention your skill as a masseur at a party. More than likely the gorgeous young lady you've been plying with drinks, dope and flattery for the last half hour will counter with, 'I've had plenty of backrubs. They're nice if you like that sort of thing but I find them rather repetitious and boring after awhile—don't you?' Look her straight in the eye, take her hand in both of yours, and coolly rotate her bones.

Hold the hand the same way you did for kneading but with thumbs pressed along the sides. Press firmly with the fingers and thumbs so that your hands do not slip. Holding firm, rotate your hands in small opposing vertical circles. When one hand is down the other should be up. You can feel the bones moving. ❧

Flexing the Hand—Backwards

Bend the hand backwards slowly until you feel resistance. Hesitate at this point and return slowly. The fingers bend out first followed by the lower hand. Use this stroke to loosen up stiff fingers as well as to stimulate the muscles of the forearm.

Forward

To flex the hand forward you bend it at the wrist. Do this by bending the arm at the elbow and grasping the hand with both thumbs at the wrist. Press down sharply with both thumbs as if you were going to drain the forearm. The thumbs need not actually move down the arm because the compression against these muscles will cause the hand to bend over as far as it will go.

❦

Pressing and Pulling the Fingers

Fingers take a little extra time to massage. Spend the time. While you're not relaxing any important muscles as you did on the upper arm the fingers are full of delicate nerve endings. A great deal of what you feel is felt through your fingers and because of this they are particularly sensitive to massage.

Begin with the little finger and work over to the thumb. Strokes are the same for each finger. Grasp the finger with your thumb and forefinger at the base and pull up the sides in short strokes to the tip. At the tip reverse the process. Work back to the base and then reverse once again. After you have moved up and down the finger four times pull it gently from the tip. Remember to stay on the sides of the fingers. The nerves there are far more sensitive than at the top and bottom. ❦

Palm Pressing

Although you work this movement just on the inside of the palm it effects both sides of the hand. While you stimulate the muscles of the palm, the bones of the top of the hand are articulated.

Hold the top of the hand firmly with all four fingers of each hand and press down into the palm with both thumbs. Move back and forth until you have covered the entire palm twice. Palm pressing relaxes the muscles that cause writer's cramp.

Thumb Kneading

Palmists believe that the thumb repre-
sents the will. Whatever its psychic significance the thumb is one of the most
active parts of the hand and deserves
extra attention during a massage. Begin
your kneading strokes on the fleshy
part of the palm where the thumb muscles are rooted. Work up slowly to the
joint and finish by pulling up the thumb
itself the same way you did when you
pulled the fingers.

    After you have massaged the thumb,
begin stroking your partner's other arm
and then do the other hand.

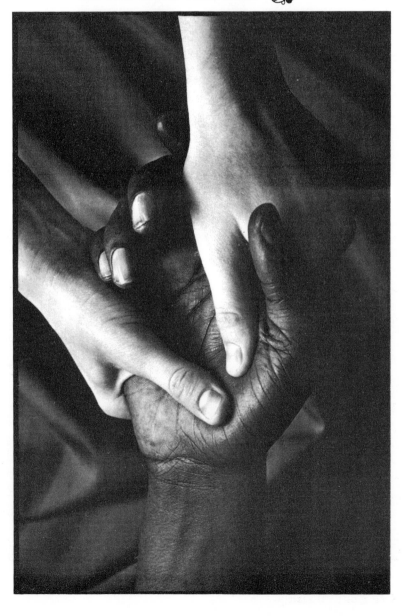

{The Front of the Legs}

Circulation

Since the legs, like the arms, take the
blood a long way from the heart it's
best to begin massaging them with a
stroke which will stimulate circulation.
The circulation pattern on the legs is
identical to the one you used on the
arms. Spread oil as you work; if your

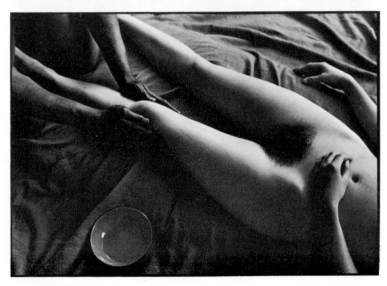

62 *A Complete Body Massage*

partner's legs are hairy, a bit more oil may be required.

On the legs begin just above the foot and turn at the top of the thighs. Lean forward with the stroke. Massage the legs with one long sweeping uninterrupted motion. Turn your hands at the top of the thigh and return pressing the sides of the leg just as you pressed the side of the arm. 🌿

Draining the Leg Below the Knee

Drain the blood from the lower leg by pressing it up towards the heart. Begin at the ankle with the hands pressing both sides of the leg as in the photograph below. Use a fair amount of pressure on the sides of the leg and work up to the knee. Depress the flesh with your hands and press it forward above the index finger. Then turn at the knee and return to the ankle. Easy, very easy—you're barely touching the sides of the leg to return and drain again. Despite the variations in pressure required for draining the leg you'll find that if you run through it a few times the entire stroke will come off as a single smooth motion. Some people say that sexual tension tightens the lower leg. Watch your partner's expression while you're draining. When you reach the knee at the top of the last draining stroke move right into circling the knee without breaking your motion. 🌿

Circling the Knee

The kneecap is shaped like a mushroom cap. Circle just under the edge of the cap with your thumbs. Hold the back of the leg with your fingers intertwined basket-style and circle the kneecap with the thumbs of each hand. You can feel the kneecap move a bit as you circle it. 🍀

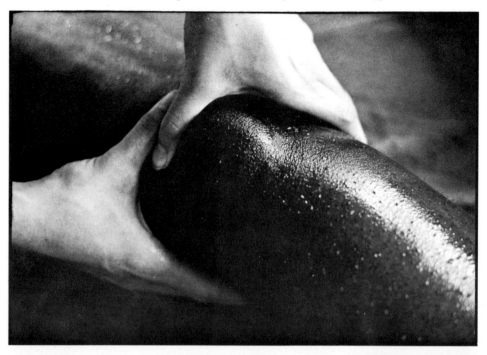

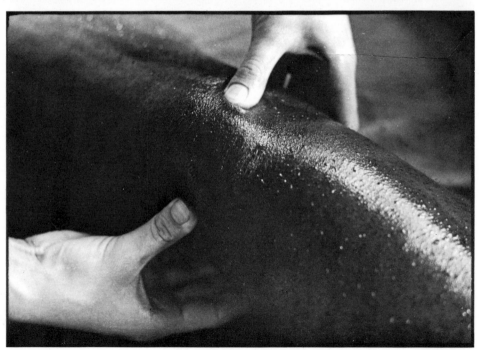

Fast Stroking the Knee

After you've done your first hundred massages you'll be amazed at the number of sprained, twisted, banged up, and generally abused knees you've had in your hands. Unless the injury is serious, like a fracture or dislocation, fast stroking will very often bring an enormous amount of relief in less than a minute. Hold your partner's leg behind the knee with the four fingers of each hand. The fingers should be together, one hand over the other. Press the thumbs in just under the kneecap, the same place you pressed for circling the knee. Work the hands and thumbs back and forth like opposing pistons. Start slowly and work up your speed until you're moving as fast as you can. Stroke at top speed for at least a half a minute and don't be surprised if your partner lets out a long sigh at the end.

Draining the Thighs

Drain the thighs with exactly the same stroke you used for the lower legs. There is more flesh here so don't be afraid to use plenty of pressure. Work from the top of the knee to the top of the leg. And at the top of the last draining stroke move right into Kneading the Leg. ❧

Kneading the Leg

Knead the leg with the same movement you used on the chest and arms. Work the leg from the top of the thigh to the ankle. Use generous strokes and pick up plenty of flesh when you knead the fleshy parts of the thigh. On the lower leg, especially near the ankle, restrict the stroke to superficial fingertip kneading. Remember that kneading is a particularly valuable stroke for breaking up fat deposits. Move up and down the leg at least three times. ❧

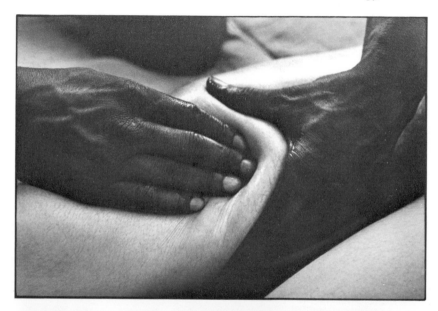

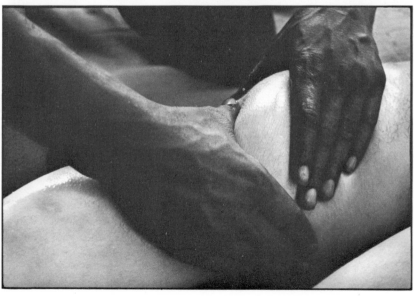

Hand over Hand pulling

Use plenty of oil and work from the top of the leg to the ankle. Your hands descend on opposite sides of your partner's leg. Grab lightly as you pull. Pull in a quickly alternating pattern (l,r,l,r,) and gradually build up speed until you're moving very fast. Use short strokes. Vary the speed constantly if you like. Hand over hand pulling feels like dozens of hands working the leg at once when it builds up speed. A thriller.

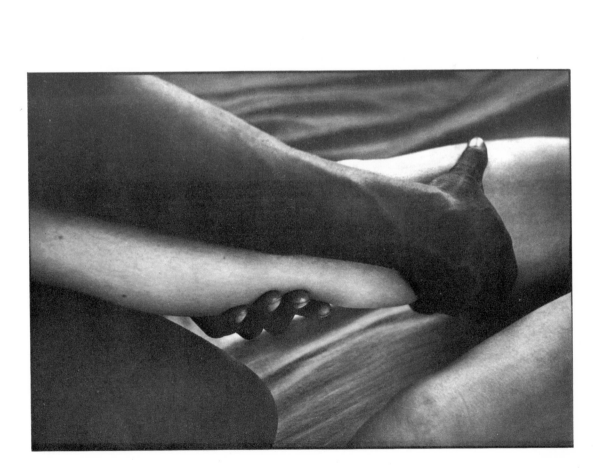

The Forearm Twist

Flex your partner's leg by lifting slowly under the knee and at the ankle. You do the work of lifting; let him relax. Steady the lower leg at the ankle with your right hand and rotate your left forearm against the limp calf muscle and tendon. Rotate three times in each direction and then reverse the action of the stroke. Steady the same foot with your left hand and rotate the right forearm against your partner's calf.

Feel the relaxed muscle roll against your smooth arms.

You may want to vary this movement by rotating your forearm on your partner's thigh as in the photograph.

The Leg Lift

The Leg Lift is a very slow-moving
stroke. Lift the legs behind the ankles,
turn them in a small circle once in each
direction, and lower them slowly. ❦

Pumping the Leg

Now that you've stroked and kneaded the entire leg from ankle to thigh, the large muscles that take the punishment of walking and lifting will be a good deal more relaxed than when you began. Never pump a tense leg. Relax the muscles individually and then pump the entire leg. Hold the right ankle with the right hand and pump with the left forearm as in the photograph.

Pump three times to the point of resistance. If the muscles are very supple the leg may flex easily to the extreme position illustrated. (The lady in the photograph is a professional belly dancer). If the leg will not bend that far press only to the point of tension. When you reach the point of tension the last time you pump, give the leg an easy extra push to stretch the muscles out a bit. ꙮ

Brushing the Legs

Finish your massage of the front of the legs by brushing from hips to toes. Brush the legs the same way you worked the arms—long rhythmic strokes. Let your body sway with the movement. ꙮ

After you have massaged one leg,
work on the other leg. Then begin the
feet.

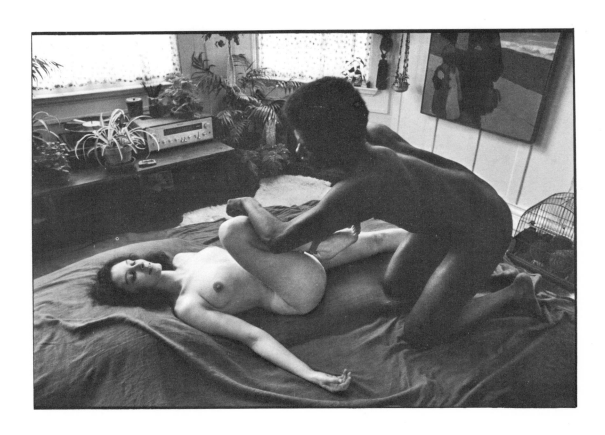

{ *The Feet* }

The puritanical crusade for better posture that has tortured most of us since childhood has done some strange things to our feet. Since they support the entire body, feet take the greatest amount of punishment while people concentrate on forcing themselves into some arbitrarily 'correct' posture. One occasionally heard argument maintains that since Indians stand and walk with their feet straight ahead this is the 'natural' way. Tibetan mountain people stand and walk with their feet turned sharply outward to hold a grip on steep surfaces. Modern shoes, like modern cars, emphasize style and tend to ignore the fact that human beings must somehow fit inside of them. Look closely at your foot after it has spent ten hours inside a pair of tight leather shoes. The toes are usually squashed, perhaps slightly blistered, the veins and capillaries are pressed flat, and the complexion resembles that of a dead fish—it feels like one too. If people bound and gagged the entire body the way they do their feet, none of us would live to the age of twenty.

Foot strokes by themselves are a fine way to relax a friend at the end of a long day. If you do decide to use the strokes in this chapter to build a comprehensive foot massage try to get your friend to lay down before you begin. It's always best to relax the entire body before you begin working on any part of it. ❧

Circulation

As you develop a personal massage style you may mix up the sequence of some of these movements. However, you should always begin your work on the foot with the circulation stroke. Remember that the feet are the farthest point to which blood is carried from the heart. Even without the restrictive influence of shoes, socks, or even sandals, circulation in this part of the body is frequently sluggish.

To stimulate the venous system, and awaken the feet, stroke the top of the foot with the flat part of each hand in a circular motion from the toes to the ankle. Circulation strokes are effective on both sides of the foot and, although you spend more of your time stroking the top, the movement is somewhat easier to do on the bottom of the foot. Elevate the foot just below the ankle with one hand and stroke all the way down from the toes with the heel of the other hand. Break contact briefly at the heel and return quickly to the toes to repeat the stroke. Circulate twenty times on the top of the foot and ten times on the bottom. 🍂

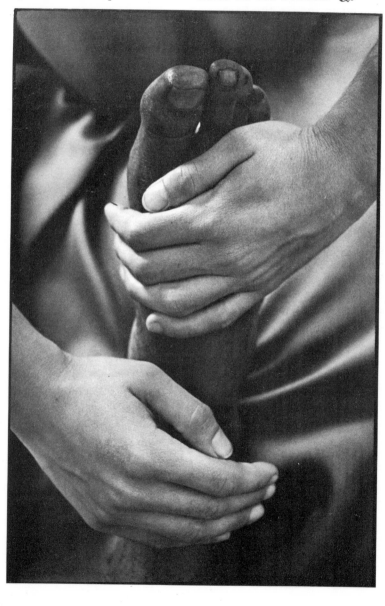

Rotating the Foot

One of the effects of the self inflicted foot torture we have been talking about is that the foot loses the ability to turn gracefully at the ankle. If you're constantly twisting and spraining your ankle, look again at the shoes you've been wearing.

Hold the foot as shown and lifting it slightly with the hand on the heel, turn it slowly at the ankle. More than likely you'll feel a good bit of stiffness. Whenever you feel stiffness, turn just inside the point of resistance. After a few massages you will feel the point of resistance gradually begin to recede. Rotate slowly three times in each direction. ❧

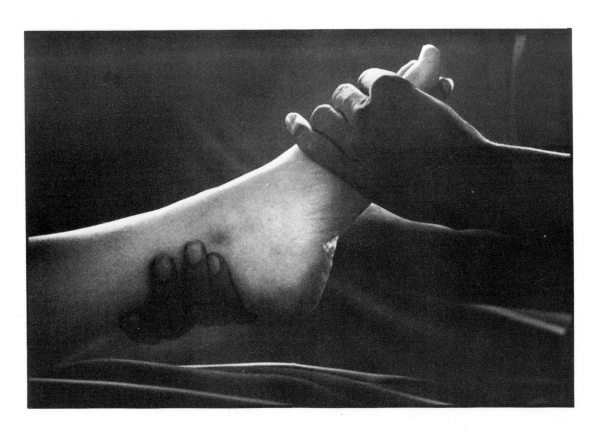

Stroking the Foot and Ankle

Oil the foot along the top and around the ankle. Although this stroke involves a number of turns, with practice you'll be able to glide through it in a single smooth motion. Press down on the foot with all four fingers of each hand just below the toes. The thumbs overlap at the beginning of the stroke and separate lower on the foot. Press down between the bones of the foot with your fingers as you work towards the ankle. At the base of the foot the fingers separate circling the ankle and return along the top of the foot to the original position (shown below). ❧

Circling the Ankles

Oil and circle the ankle with the four fingers of each hand. As you circle vary the pressure and speed of your stroke. Be careful to stay off of the ankle itself but work as close as possible to it. You may want to change the direction of the movement. As you end, move as fast as possible and hold your speed for five seconds. ❧

Foot Pulling

Hold the foot firmly with both hands as shown. Lift it just an inch or so and pull sharply. Sharply, not violently. One pull for each foot is fine. This simple stroke not only exercises the ankle but it works on the large joint where the hip and leg are joined. ❧

Kneading the Top of the Foot

You knead the top of the foot the same way you kneaded the back of the hand. Its easier here because you've got the fleshy bottom of the foot to hold onto. Feel the bones and tendons ripple as you rotate your thumbs up from the ankle to the toes. ❧

Flexing and Rotating the Bones of the Foot

Once again, these movements are identical to the ones you used on the hand. Since the bones here are longer and somewhat thicker, and the muscles are more resistant, flexing takes quite a bit more pressure than it did on the hand.

Press outward with the heel of each hand and inward and up with the fingertips. For rotation hold the same position and rotate the hands in opposing circles. (Remember that one hand should be up while the other is down). If you have tiny hands and you're massaging huge feet you may have some difficulty in moving the interior bones. Don't let it bother you. This is one of the very few movements where the size of your hands makes any difference. ❧

Pressing the Arch

A good bit of the fatigue people complain about in their feet centers around the metatarsal arch. This stroke reverses the direction of the enormous tension that the arch must often bear. The stroke follows the same movement pattern as bottom of the foot circulation. The difference here is in your treatment of the arch itself.

Press up along the arch with the heel of your hand as you pass over it. Use plenty of pressure. This part of the foot can bear it. Be careful not to allow the extra pressure you're exerting on the arch interfere with the rhythm of the stroke. ❧

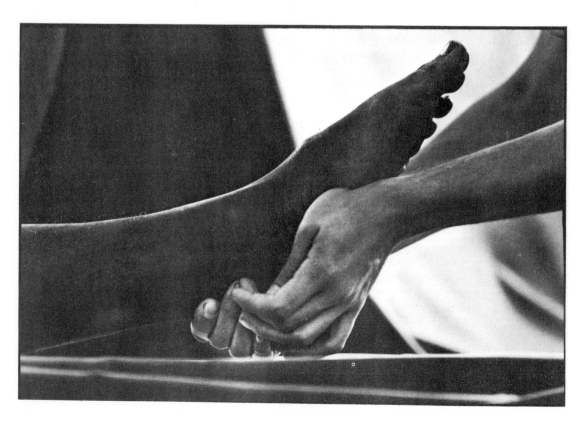

Flexing, Stroking, Rotating, and Pulling the Toes

When was the last time you had your toes individually flexed, stroked, rotated, and pulled? Do you realize that this is the kind of thing that used to go on every day in the bath houses of Rome and Egypt? *What happened?*

Toes, like fingers, are marvelously sensitive to touch. Go through the entire cycle of toe strokes on each toe beginning with the little toe. Flex by bending the toe over a rigid finger. Stroke with your fingertips up and down the sides of the toe where the nerves are thickest. Grasp the sides of the toe and rotate slowly three times in both directions. End your toe massage by grasping all the toes, as shown, and flexing them up and down five times. ❧

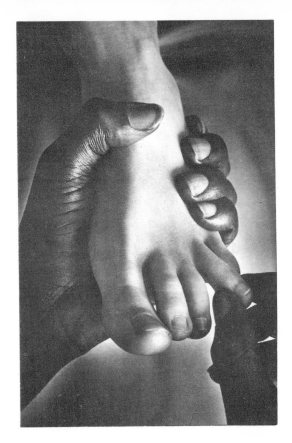

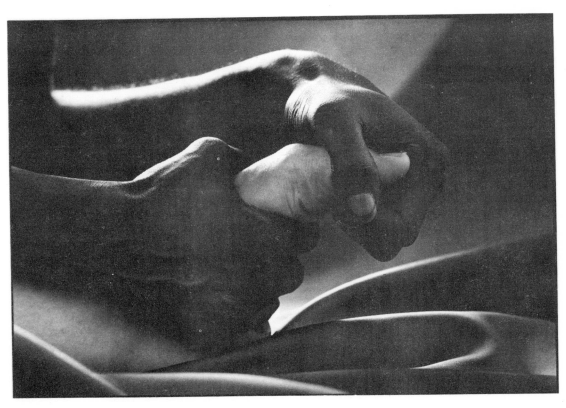

Kneading the Bottom of the Foot

Knead the bottom of the foot the same way you kneaded the top. Raise the leg just a bit or support it with a pillow and knead in a deep circular motion with both thumbs. Cover the entire bottom of the foot.

At the end of foot massage your partner turns over so you can begin stroking the back of the legs and back. Some people like to knead the bottom of the foot once again from this new perspective. It feels good and that's all the justification you need for introducing a new stroke into your massage technique. Grasp the top of the foot with the four fingers of each hand and deep knead the arch and heel with both thumbs. ✿

Turning and Squeezing the Heel

Rotate the three middle fingers around the heel of the foot. Begin moving around the outside of the heel and slowly decrease the circles of rotation until you are pressing on the center of the heel. Finish by squeezing all around the outside of the heel with your fingertips.

✿

Stroking the Achilles Tendon

The achilles tendon, the thick muscle that rises just behind the ankle, is used in almost every foot action. To relax it, kneel along the side of your partner's leg, bend your wrists and press both index fingers against the back of the leg. Support the index finger with your other fingers and rotate your hands up along this long thin muscle (as in the photograph on the facing page). You may want to extend this movement up the leg a bit to where this tendon merges with the larger muscles of the calf. When you finish massaging the feet, wipe the oil off the entire front surface of your partner's body. You may want to use alcohol (see page 3) particularly if you're working on a hairy man. Use a soft towel and move slowly, gently. This gentle rubdown, like everything else you do with your hands, should become part of the massage. Don't try to get every drop of oil off the skin. Up and down the body once with the towel is fine. ✿

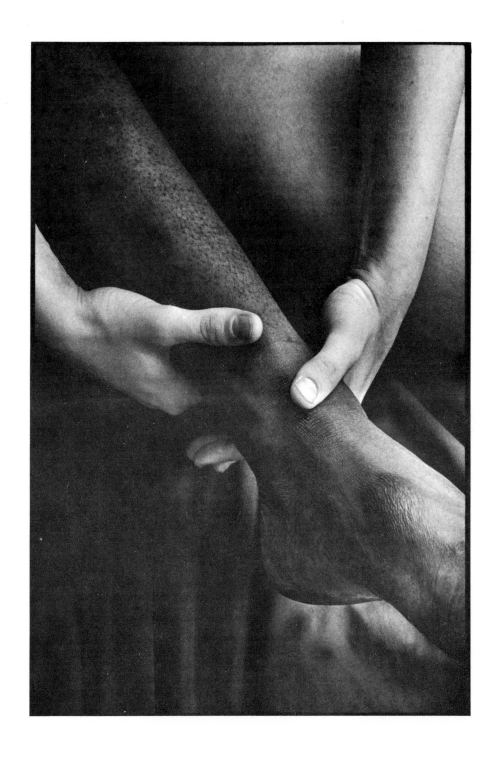

{The Back of the Legs}

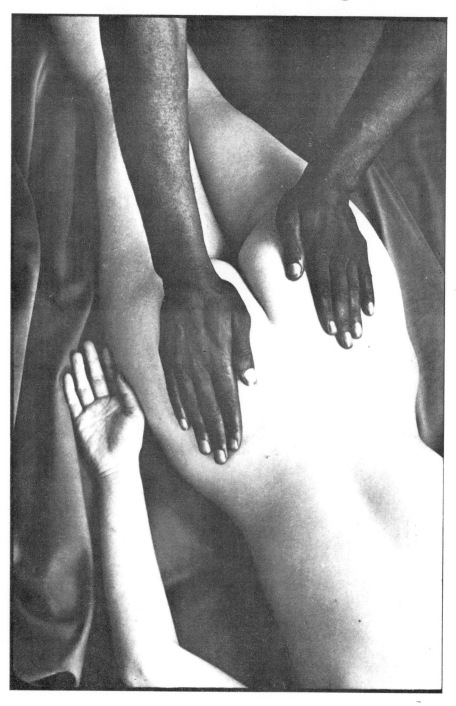

The back of the legs take several of the strokes you used on the front of the legs. Because there's more flesh to work with here movements will penetrate more deeply. Ask your partner to turn over. It's the only thing you'll ask of him throughout the massage. If you're working on the ground or floor, lay the arms at the side palms up. If you have to move the arms or legs use both hands to do it. That way you avoid jerking or pulling them. The feet should be far enough apart to permit you to knead the inside of the thigh. ❧

Circulation

Circulation, kneading and draining operate the same way here as they did on the front of the leg. Since you don't have to worry about pressing on bones on the lower part of the leg you can use somewhat more pressure here as you spread the oil and begin stroking. Glide over the back of the knee in a single uninterrupted motion. ❧

Draining the Lower Leg

Like circulation, draining is a good bit easier on this side of the leg because you can press down directly on the center of the muscle rather than having to distribute pressure on the sides of the leg. Press tension out of the leg as you work up towards the knee. Sexual tension, nervous tension, fatigue. Drain this part of the leg fifteen times. ❧

Rotating on the Back of the Knee

Press one palm on the back of the knee and press on the top of that hand with the palm of the other hand (as in the photograph below). Pressing moderately hard with both hands, rotate your palm slowly five times in each direction on the back of the knee. There's a special problem here if you're working with hairy men (or women). Hair, even well oiled hair, will knot up if you rotate on it. Modify the stroke so that only the flesh of the back of the knee moves as you turn your hand. Do this by pressing a little harder and inscribing only a tiny circle as you move. The effect on the muscles of the back of the knee will be about the same. ❧

Draining the Thighs

The heaviest fat concentrations are on this side of the leg. Sometimes you can feel them rippling unevenly against your fingers as you drain. If 'reducing' is part of the massage plan you might double the usual ten strokes for this part of the body. ❧

Kneading the Back of the Leg

Knead, again, from the side of the leg. There's more flesh to work with and less bony resistance at the knee to break up the motion. Stroke deeply on the thighs flattening out as you move onto the lower part of the leg. Work up and down the leg three times. ❧

Rotating the Lower Leg

Flatten the palm of one hand against the back of the knee to steady the thigh and grasp the leg at the ankle. Raise the foot and rotate three times in each direction. ❧

Flexing the Leg

This movement begins with the same position you used to begin rotating the leg. When the foot is upright pump it backwards to the point of resistance. The point of resistance will vary greatly from one person to another. Sometimes athletes and dancers will show no resistance and the foot actually touches the buttocks. On older people, though, the point is often reached just a few inches back from the vertical position. Pump to this point four times. On the fifth stroke thrust suddenly just a hair beyond the point of resistance. This simple exercise stretches the tightened muscles. Work on this leg a day or two later and you may find that it stretches just a bit farther. 🍀

Back Leg Lift

Lift at the ankles while you steady the legs above the knees. Turn once in each direction, slowly in a large circle, the same way you did on the front of the legs (shown below). 🍀

Buttock Rotation—Fast and Slow

Fast

This is one of those massage strokes that almost everyone already knows. Rotate the palms and closed fingers of each hand on the buttocks. One hand for each side. Vary the direction, the speed, and the pressure as you like. After about fifteen seconds rotate as fast as you can for a final five second burst. ❧

Slow

Feel for the indentation in the pelvic bones, one hand on the back of the other, fingers closed. Press into the indentation and rotate the way you would on the back of a hairy knee, moving the flesh rather than your hands. Five times in each direction. End the stroke by pressing sharply into the indentation a single time on each side. ❧

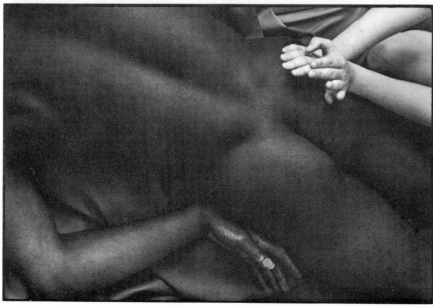

{ *The Back* }

The back is the most important part of any full body massage. Usually you will spend more than a third of your time here. Decent back massage requires a fair amount of effort—expect to work up a sweat before you're done.

The spinal area is the core of the entire nervous system. Anxiety or nervous tension are very often caused by nothing more than tight, sore muscles around the spine. When you relax the back it's not unusual to find that a great many supposedly psychological problems have vanished. Every moment of your life your body is an extension of your mind. You are what you feel.

Center your back strokes at the two ends of the spine. Working from the bottom of the spine you will find it easier if you kneel astride your partner. Even if you're using a table the astride position distributes pressures more evenly and gives you better leverage for this part of the massage. Between strokes you can rest briefly by sitting back lightly on your partner's thighs.

The muscles of the back are massaged in three groups: the long muscles that run parallel to the spine, the flat muscle groups that cover the top of the back and the lower neck, and the wide band of muscles that stretches from the spine to the side of the back. Begin with a simple circulation stroke that will stimulate all three areas in a single easy sweep.

Circulation

Circulation on the back works very
much the way it did on the abdomen.
Begn with your hands flat, fingers facing (but not touching) the spine on the
lower back. Press up the back to the
neck where you turn, circle the
shoulders, and return, fingers pressing
the sides. Turn once again at the waist
and return to the original position.
Enjoy the smoothness of your partner's
back while you glide across it,

Repeat the circulation movement ten
times. The last few times through you
might want to vary it by rotating your
hands in tiny circles as you return along
the sides of the back. ❧

Pressing the Back

Pressing the back is probably the single most dramatic stroke in massage. Like circulation, back pressing engages all three of the large muscle groups. In a few impressive passes it can relax a massive part of the body, the center of the back. At the same time it stimulates the spinal nerve bundle. Because of the direct connection between the spine and all internal organs, some medical men believe that massaging this area profoundly affects the health of the entire body. Watch your partner shudder and moan with delight when you press up along the spine.

Start at the base of the spine using the heel of each hand. Press up moderately hard along the parallel ridges of muscles and into the indentation next to the spinal cord itself. Lean forward as you press. Turn at the shoulder blades and return as you did in the circulation stroke, except this time work the thumb into the indentation between spine and muscle. Lift up along the sides, when you return. Repeat this basic back press ten times before you begin any variations.

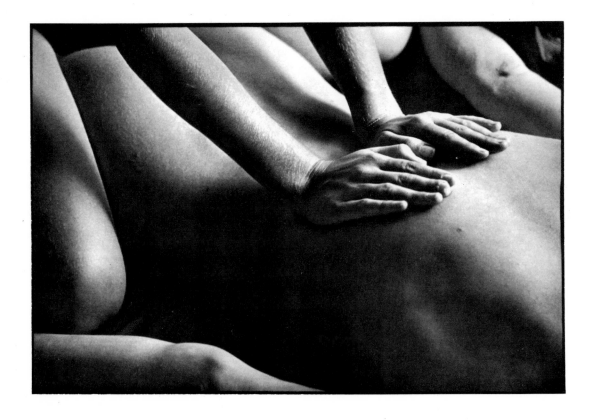

Very often one side of the back is somewhat stiffer than the other. Concentrate all your pressure on the stiff side by pressing just that side with one hand on top of the other (see page 85, Rotating on the Back of the Knee).

You can use the thumbs along the spine on the press stroke as well as on the return. Work them along the spine, as shown in the photograph, when you press up the back. Feel the vertabrae roll off the end of your thumb but concentrate most of your pressure in the valley between muscle and spine. Separate your hands at the neck and return the same way you did in the basic stroke. Even after the first ten strokes go through each variation of this movement at least five times.

[Rhythm Breathing]

We use the word partner to describe the person you're stroking because massage is a *shared* experience; you look beautiful together. By now you can see that giving pleasure with your hands this way is a kind of dance. One partner is active, the other passive—two bodies moving together in time and pleasure.

When you're pressing your partner's back there's a way the two of you can be closer. Pressing begins with both hands flat at the base of the spine. Hold still and feel your partner's body moving as he breathes. The back rises and falls evenly, rhythmically. Without moving up the back press your hands down with each exhalation and let them rise as breath is taken in. When you feel the rhythm ask your partner to exaggerate his breathing. Once again feel the back moving. All life is motion. Let your partner take a deep breath and press up the back. Push the air out of his lungs. Turn at the top of the back and, when he begins to inhale, pull back up along the sides. Press down again into the stroke when he begins to exhale. You can follow the breathing and massage with your own breathing until you're in time with your partner. Dance together to the oldest rhythm: breath. ❧

Spine Ripple and Intervertebral Flutter

The next three movements work directly on the spine itself.

The Press—Press up the spine with the heel of your hand using the familiar hand over hand technique. You'll feel the spine bubbling against the heel of your hand as you move very slowly to the neck. Separate and return as you did in Back Pressing.

The Crab—Arch your hand and press down on the spine with the heel of your hand while you push along (and against) the spine with two fingers. Move up and down the spine ten times like this.

The Rocking Chair—The Rocking Chair combines both of the last two movements. Go up the spine the way you did in the Press. Return, pushing on either side of the spine with two fingers as in the Crab. Sometimes it seems like you're not doing much with these movements. You can't feel the spectacular effects on the nervous system but your partner can. 🍀

Fingertip Kneading the Long Muscles Along the Spine

You used fingertip kneading across the abdomen. The same movement will release tension and spread pleasure along the spine. Powerfully built men always enjoy this stroke. 🍀

Back Compression [Hands Together]

Press the heel of each hand against the long ridge of muscles that run parallel to either side of the spine. The position is as easy as it looks in the photograph. Flatten the four fingers of each hand over the muscle swell and press moderately hard. Move along the spine from neck to waist compressing this large muscle group with both hands. Unless your partner is unusually tense you will feel the muscles give a bit while you massage. The usual three passes up and down the back has a marvelously soothing effect on the entire torso under your hands. ❧

Back Compression [Hands Opposed]

Some people love to have their backs compressed. You'll hear them sighing loudly as you literally push the wind out of their lungs. Here's an easy variation you can add to extend your technique for compression lovers.

Work the same long muscles as before. But in this stroke press on both sides of the back at once. Do this by positioning your hands with the heels opposite each other as shown. This measure distributes the pressures more evenly and is particularly useful if you're massaging someone much smaller than yourself. When you compress both sides of the back evenly you avoid the occasional tendency to 'shove' your partner to one side when you press. ❧

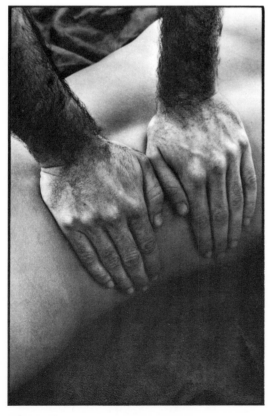

Deep Stroking the Back

Deep Stroking is easy to learn, but like most of the other back movements it takes some work to bring it off effectively. Once again, use the hand over hand position to concentrate pressure. Press the fleshy part of the back and avoid the central spine this time. While you press, rotate your hands in small circles. Massage all of your partner's back with this smooth easy motion. Begin at the bottom of the back and move up slowly—be careful not to miss any spot between the waist and shoulders. Cross at the neck (light pressure here and over the shoulder blades) and again at the base of the spine. As you cross it, rotate three times on the bony base of the spine using moderate pressure. After you've rotated on the base of the spine, circle the back once again in the opposite direction. Circle the back four times reversing your stroke each time on the base of the spine. ✤

Swimming

Swim over the entire back from waist to shoulders. Use the same motion here that you used on the chest and abdomen. Easy on the shoulder blades. Move up and down the back four times. 🌿

Kneading the Back

Knead both sides of the back exactly the same way you kneaded the chest and legs. It's easier going here than on the chest because you always have more flesh to stroke. Knead from the hip to the underarm and this time don't hesitate to lift and press the muscles when you feel them. Work up and down each side of the back five times. 🌿

The Scissors

Press folds of flesh with the thumb of
one hand into the 'scissors' formed between the thumb and forefinger of the
other hand. Slide your hands up and
down both sides of your partner's back
until you have covered the same areas
you massaged in Deep Stroking. It's
best not to jump around. The scissors is
more effective if it moves methodically,
a little at a time. Once over the back
will do.

The Forearm Press

Press down on your forearm with your hand. Rotate your forearm in small circles while you stroke up and down the back four times. ❧

Reversal of Back Strokes

Circulation, Back Pressing, and the spine movements feel just as good starting at the top of the spine as they did when you started at the bottom. Kneeling at your partner's head work through each of these movements again from the top of the back. ❧

Rotating the Shoulder

By lifting just under your partner's
shoulder with one hand and steadying
the shoulder blade with the other, you
can rotate the entire shoulder. (Actually, you're rotating the shoulder blade
and the shoulder.) Press firmly with
both hands to hold a smooth even
motion. Turn in a small horizontal arc.

After the third rotation keep the
shoulder elevated and, with your top
hand, stroke around the shoulder blade
three times.

You can vary this stroke by lifting
under your partner's flexed arm. Steady
the flexed arm with your free hand
while you lift to the point of tension.

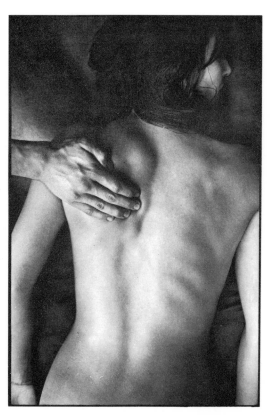

Shoulder Curling

This stroke can be rather delicate if your partner has thin shoulders. To master it, work slowly, so you can feel the flesh around the bones of the shoulder. Press up from just beneath the shoulder blades with your hands flat. Slide lightly over the shoulder blades and curl your fingers over the ridge of the shoulder. As you curl your fingertips over the shoulder, press your heel up so you can fold the flesh of the shoulder between the fingertips and heel of your hand. Return by reversing the movement (shown below). 🍀

Shoulder Kneading

You can work on that tension that women feel at the base of the neck from the back as well as around the head and neck. The muscles of the upper back that actually support the neck are the ones you're concerned with here. Massage them by kneading across the top of the back. Move across the top of the back from shoulder to shoulder. 🍀

Thumb Strokes for the Lower Neck

Hold your partner's shoulders on either side of the neck and stroke up and down the lower neck with your thumbs. Use a circular thumb motion like the one you used to knead the hands and feet. 🍀

Kneading the Back of the Neck

Here is one neck stroke that you simply can't do from the other side of the body. Combine it with shoulder kneading and neck thumb strokes to complete the thorough relaxation of the upper back. Kneel at your partner's side. With your partner's head facing you, deep knead the thick muscles on the back of the neck. ❧

The Back Lift

Those readers who have had experience with wrestling will recognize the positioning of this movement as the familiar 'Half Nelson.' While wrestlers use this position to practically break their opponent's neck, we will use it to gently stretch the abdominal muscles. You don't need to be a wrestler to do this stroke, but you will need a fair amount of strength to bring it off smoothly, especially if you and your partner are on the ground. Very often it helps to raise one knee as you lift, so that your heel will give you extra balance. One try and you'll know if your back can handle it.

clasp your hands together basket style behind your partner's neck. Lift your partner until you feel resistance in the abdominal muscles. This resistance, the point of tension, is usually quite apparent at about a forty-five-degree angle to the floor. Turn and twist the body from side to side at the point of tension for a few seconds and then return slowly to the floor. Repeat the lift three times and on the top of the third lift hold the back up for a silent count of ten before returning for the final time. Follow your partner's body with your body as you lift and lower the back. 🌿

Warming the Back

Stroke up and down the back with the open part of each hand in a long slow piston motion. One hand up while the other is down. You can vary this movement by pressing the long muscles along the spine with your thumbs while you stroke. 🍃

Back and Body Brushing

Brush the spine, the back and the legs. Come off the legs onto the back of the feet and break contact between your fingertips and your partner's toes very slowly.

The massage is over.

Don't expect people to speak at the end of a massage. They are as close as they are going to get in this life to levitation. 🍃

An Extended Massage

3.

{Percussion}

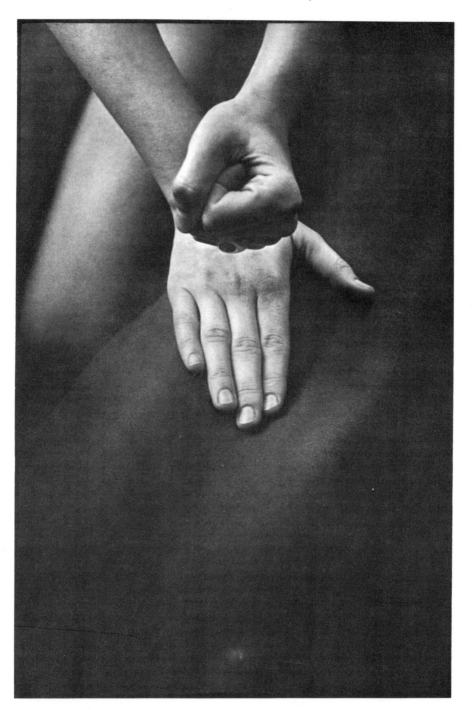

The idea that massage is painful is old and false. Techniques like Deep Zone (a folk healing process that sometimes utilizes intense pressures on the feet), and Rolfing, (an excruciatingly painful muscle treatment), have nothing at all to do with massage. Such painful 'alternatives' to established medical practice have always been with us, and were particularly popular during the sexually repressive Victorian era.

If your partner needs to be hurt he isn't looking for a massage. Massage feels good. Even the percussion movements, the so-called 'violent' strokes, are intensely sensual if they are used carefully and executed with a fair amount of restraint. Use them to bring blood to the body surface and to relax tensed muscles.

You communicate yourself when you give a massage. But a tensed body cannot feel the nuances of expression which characterize your own personal technique. Unless there is a serious problem resulting in extreme tension, fifteen minutes of percussion will begin to relax even the tightest body. Some people accept tension as a fact of life. When you remove tension by relaxing knotted back and leg muscles your partner may fall asleep halfway through the massage. Let him. It may be his best sleep in years.

The effects of fifteen minutes of percussion is really remarkable. If your partner has never experienced it, and has been depending on alcohol, tranquilizers and other drugs for relaxation, this will be the discovery of a new way to unwind.

If you plan to incorporate the percussion movements into a general massage use them at the beginning on your partner's back. Although some people like a few minutes of percussion integrated with back massage, this effect can break the smooth soothing mood of a long hour of massage. Feel your partner. If he's really tense, a few minutes of percussion as you begin massaging may help him to enjoy the next hour even more.

Pounding

After a hard day's work, or during intense emotional stress, the muscles of the back sometimes refuse to relax. As you work you will feel them soften. Pound the back of one hand with the other beginning at the base of one side of the spine. Work upward slowly, rhythmically. At the top of the spine move down the same way but double-time the blows. Work the other side of the spine and then move up and down the spinal cord itself. You can continue moving around the entire back double and even-triple timing your strokes. Pound out tightness wherever you feel it. Leaves them limp and smiling. . ❧

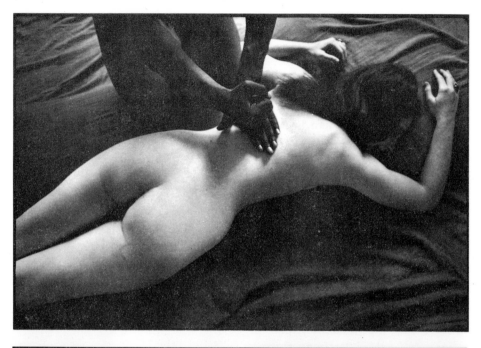

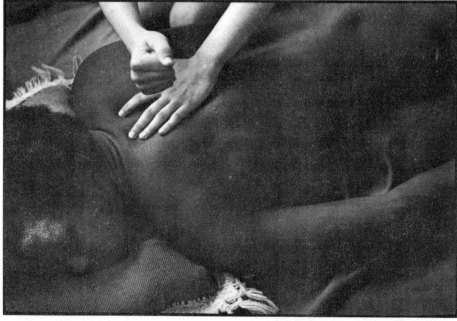

Knuckle Rapping

Knuckle rapping, a variation of pounding, is particularly useful when you wish to increase the speed of your percussion. Since you're working with two hands separately it's easy lay down a fast evenly spaced series of strokes. Pound the back, the two hands alternating quickly, with the flat part of each knuckle. Be careful not to hit the back with the sharp joint of the fingers. Work the same areas you covered with pounding but go easy on the spine. 🍂

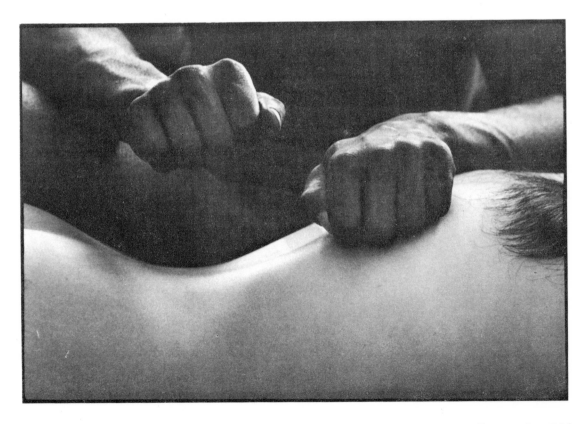

Hacking

This is the dazzling stuff you've seen in movies set in the Orient. Unlike some of the other percussion movements it works almost anywhere on the body but it feels best on the back. The second, third, and fourth fingers are held together. The little finger hangs down to partially absorb the blow. One hand hacks at a time and you should hear the little finger clicking as the hand comes down on it. Hacking is something like playing the drums. When you get it right it *sounds* smooth and even, like a well executed drum roll. Work in the same pattern as pounding but do not hack at the spine itself. Generally, most strokes should stay off the spine. 🌿

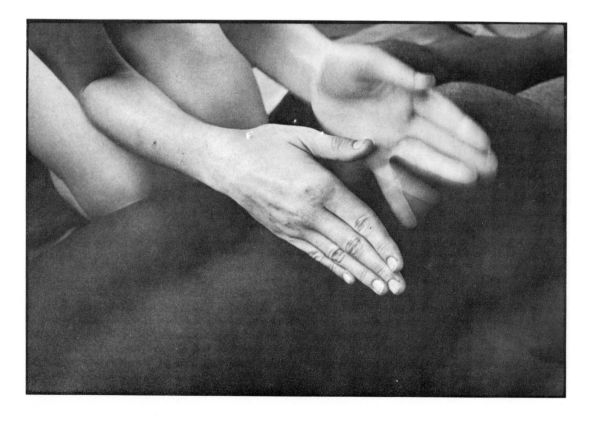

Elbow Pounding

Elbow Pounding is the most intense percussion movement. If you're partner is much bigger than you and you're wondering how to relax that immense back, this may be the answer. Use half your arm as a wedge to drive the elbow into the back muscles. Pound on the top of your fist (or if you prefer, the heel of your hand) with the palm of the other hand. Move up and down the long back muscles that run parallel to the spine but, again, stay off of the spine itself.

It's easy to overpower your partner with Elbow Pounding. Go easy. Feel what he needs and set a moderate limit on the intensity of your pounding. If you're working on a fragile body or one with chronic back problems it's best to skip this stroke entirely. 🌿

Hand Cupping

When it's done with water glasses (see Special Effects: Cupping Strokes) the cupping movement creates a partial vacuum under the glass which lifts the flesh of the back. Hand cupping can approximate the same effect over the entire back and legs. Cup the hands, fingers together, and clap them along both sides of the spine (once again follow the initial pounding pattern). You'll feel the flesh raise a bit each time you lift your hands from your partner's body. Definitely the loudest massage stroke. Use it to wake up a listless, unfeeling body. 🌿

Plucking

Tap out a light pattern over your partner's back and legs using just your fingertips. Each time you press into the back pick up a small fold of flesh and squeeze it gently. Once again, vary your speed and rhythm at both ends of the spine. Julius Caesar loved to have his back and legs plucked. It's the perfect stroke for heavily egoed types.

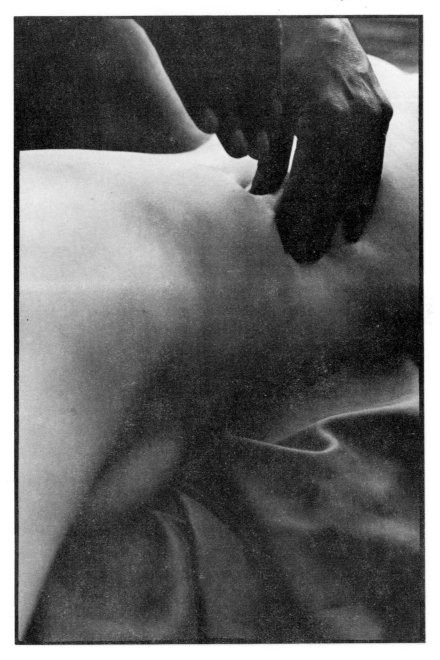

{ Special Effects }

During the course of a complete body massage your partner needs to move only once—to turn over when you finish stroking the toes. Aside from that single uncomplicated motion you do *all* the work and the body under your hands passively experiences the sensuous effects of massage.

There are, however, movements that alter the mellow vibrations of a body massage. They are not included in the general massage section of the book simply because they create moods which are quite different from the ones described there. We call them Special Effects.

There are two ways to use this part of the book. You can incorporate these strokes into your massage technique a few at a time depending on your partner's preference or you can create a separate shorter massage using only Special Effects. Since none of these movements require oil or powder they have the advantage of being adaptable to almost any situation. You may hear an occasional pop as the joints are worked into unusual positions—nothing to worry about.

Some Special Effects are quite dramatic, so if you sense that your partner has been unsettled by neck cracking or knee snapping for example, you will find that a few moments of soothing talk is calming. But remember that massage is not a verbal experience. Resist any temptation to start a long conversation. Your tone is far more important than the words you use.

Neck Cracking

If your partner has any neck or back problems neck cracking is not a good idea. In general, however, this simple quick movement can release an immense amount of tension from the neck and upper back.

The head turns from side to side in a close half circle. Begin by feeling this arc. Turn the head from side to side slowly. Experiment with the feel of the head as it turns smoothly on the neck. You aren't wasting time; people love to have their head lifted and turned. It relaxes the mind to have someone else bear the weight of the brain and skull. The exotic weightless sensation that divers and astronauts experience is very close to the floating-mind feeling of skillful head turning. Turn until the neck feels relaxed and supple.

Hold the head and neck firmly—you need close control of this movement. Grasp the top of the neck just under the base of the skull with your left hand. Hold the chin and cheek with your right hand. Turn the head slowly to the left until you feel the muscles resist. At the point of tension, stop; then give the head a *very* short jerk beyond this point. You will hear a cracking sound as the top vertebrae are articulated. If you don't hear a crack resist the temptation to try again. The neck is a very delicate part of the body and one cracking attempt on each side is enough for a massage. Try again another day.

Crack the other side of the neck by reversing the position of your hands and repeating the same procedure.

A successful neck cracking technique very often depends on your ability to sense the point of tension when you turn the neck. A quick jerk just outside the point of tension is all you need to bring off this stroke. Remember that turning the head in too large an arc will probably not work and may even hurt your partner, so practice neck cracking cautiously. Like almost any stroke, there's nothing to it once you get the hang of it. ❧

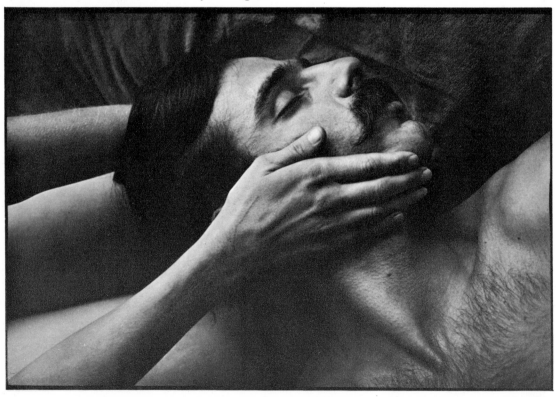

Neck Stretch

The body is full of indentations and 'handles' that make massage easy. One of them, the indentation at the base of the skull behind the ears, is perfectly situated for stretching the neck. Press into this space with the heel of one hand while you hold the shoulder with the other hand. Steady your partner at the shoulder while you stretch the neck to the point of tension by pressing that skull indentation with the heel of your hand. Stretch the neck three times on each side. Gentle stretching here is all you need. Brush the sides of the neck with your fingertips after you stretch. People love to have their necks brushed.

The Neck Lift

The neck lift is a magnificent-looking stroke. Fold your hands, one over the other, under the neck palms up. As you lift to about six inches watch the head fall back passionately. Hold for a count of ten and lower the neck very slowly. The neck lift feels as good as it looks.

The Back Twist

Once again, be sure your partner has
no serious back problems if you plan to
try the back twist. This movement articulates the pelvic girdle and adjusts the
spinal column. Work from the shoulder
and the hips and your partner will feel
tension easing evenly along the entire
spine. Press toward you with the side of
your elbow against the hips as shown in
the photograph. At the same time exert
the same amount of pressure on your
partner's shoulder pushing away from
you. Press slowly and gently just
beyond the point of tension three times.
As you watch the back twist gracefully
between your hands you may see that
slow spreading smile so familiar to experienced masseurs. 🥀

Chest Stretch

The chest stretch is a fine movement for women who are concerned with lifting and firming their busts. Use it on men to strengthen the long muscles of the upper torso. With your partner lying on one side, facing away from you reach around under the arm and press the palm of your hand against the middle of the back. Steady the body with your left hand against the small of the back and press down against your partner's arm with your right arm. As you bend the arm back, the chest muscles tighten. Press just past the point of tension, hold for a few moments, and release slowly. Usually you will stretch the chest three times on each side, but if you're working on a specific problem (like firming the bust) begin with six chest stretch strokes and work up to twenty gradually as you massage from day to day. This way the chest stretch, like several other special effects, can be used as an effective 'passive exercise.' 🌿

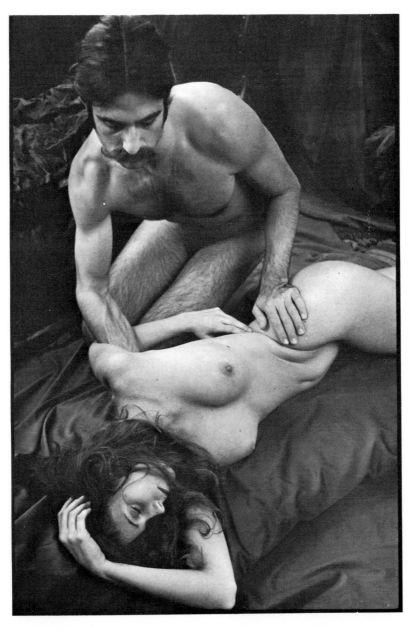

The Back Stretch

Here is a simple back adjustment that will very often relieve discomfort in the shoulder girdle and hip at the same time. Press up on the underside of the shoulder blade with the heel of one hand. At the same time press down on the crest of the opposite hip bone with the heel of the other hand. Both these bones are usually quite prominent and you can feel them easily. Remember you're touching just the side of each bone. Avoid pressing down on either hip or shoulder blade. Stretch the back three times on each side. 🌿

Flexing the Arms

Fold the palms of each hand in turn, up
over the shoulder, as in the photograph,
and hold the arm below the elbow and
at your partner's shoulder. Use the
hand at the shoulder to steady the arm
while you lift and rotate it from below
the elbow. Rotate three times in each
direction and then press the arm up to
the point of tension three times. This
simple stroke exercises muscles on both
sides of the upper arm. Arm flexing is
particularly pleasurable for people who
do a great deal of heavy lifting. 🌿

The Elbow Lift

Since the top of the back is such a common source of tension, your partner will appreciate it if you give it extra attention during a massage. When you're working on someone who complains of tension at the base of the neck, it's a simple trick to incorporate the elbow lift into a general back massage. It isn't included in the general massage section only because it involves extra rearranging of arms and hands.

Fold your partner's hands, palms down, under the neck. Lift both elbows a few inches and pull them back to the point of tension. Lift and pull back four times to stretch muscles of the upper back and the underarm. The elbow lift is one of those movements that may make your partner moan softly. It feels that good. ❧

The Full Leg Press

The full leg press stretches and exercises the hamstring muscles that run along the back of the leg from the buttocks to the knee. Once again you and your partner move your bodies together to execute this movement. Pay the same close attention to your partner's body now that you would if you were dancing together. Kneeling, press both your legs against the inside thigh and calf and push forward against the entire leg. Flex the whole leg to the point of tension by moving forward against it slowly. On the third and final press hold, once again, for a silent count of ten and back off slowly. 🌿

Pressing the Arms

Press each arm in turn across your partner's chest until you feel the muscles tighten. Be sure to hold the arm with both hands when you return to give it plenty of support. ❧

The Shoulder Lift

Hold your partner gently along the side of the head while you twist behind the arm as in the photograph below. With both hands firmly in place lean forward slowly and feel the shoulder lift as you move. ❧

The Knee Snap

The knee snap is one of those rare movements where you need your partner's help. Hold the knees about six inches apart and ask your partner to resist by pressing the knees together as hard as possible. Let muscle tension build while you continue to hold the legs apart despite your partner's resistance. After a quarter of a minute release the knees suddenly and they will snap together sharply. This sudden snapping motion at the knee articulates the joint at the top of the leg. One snap is all you need. ❧

Stretching the Thigh

To stretch the thigh you must literally wrap yourself around it. Twist your hand and arm around your partner's thigh. Use your other arm to steady your partner. Do this by pressing the flat of your hand into the small of the back. As you lean slowly to the side the entire leg from hip to foot will rise with you. Press it up to the point of tension four times. ❧

Brushes

Most hairy men don't know how great it feels to have their backs and chest brushed. Use a small brush with flexible, bristles and brush the hair in rhythmic patterns, which you invent and vary as you feel with your partner. A plastic baby brush or a soft hair brush works well. Avoid stiff bristled brushes. Try pounding lightly over his back and legs after you've finished brushing. Men particularly appreciate brushing just before their bodies are rubbed down with alcohol. ❧

Rollers

Rubber rollers or a household rolling pin up and down the back and legs . . . yes. ❧

The Vibrator

Although we generally discourage the use of gadgets, the effects of a vibrator simply cannot be duplicated with bare hands. A good one will cost between twenty-five and fifty dollars. Owning a vibrator makes you glad you were born in the twentieth century.

Strap the vibrator on as follows. Place your two middle fingers through the first loop and all four fingers through the second. Strap the outside band of the second loop around the base of your thumb to steady the machine on your hand. Keep the cord away from the massage area.

Work the entire body. Use your fingertips where you can't easily press with the flat of the hand. Vibrators create such a rush that it almost doesn't matter what you do at first. When you settle down, concentrate on the scalp, the back of the neck, the spine, (using your fingertips), and the feet. Some masseurs like to begin a general mas-sage with a massive five minutes of electric vibration. The ladies definitely dig it. If it's her first massage she may be surprised to find that the vibrator treatment isn't the whole massage. But if she really loves the vibrator there is something more you can do for her. Get another one for your other hand. 🍂

Chinese Hot Cupping

For at least the last twenty-five-hundred years Chinese physicians have used cupping with animal horns, bamboo tubes, bells, and burnt clay pots to treat colds, diarrhea, headaches, abdominal pains and a number of other ailments. The most recent application of this strange technique utilizes an ordinary glass tumbler to raise the flesh and open the pores just about anywhere on the body where there is a soft expanse. Here's how it works:

Burn some oil or alcohol soaked cotton in a three inch tumbler. Remove the burning cotton when the glass starts to get very hot. Allow the tumbler to cool just enough so that it can be placed mouth down on the body. As the air inside the glass cools it contracts exerting a powerful suction force on the skin. The flesh rises quite dramatically into the cup. Ten or fifteen minutes later tip the cup (or cups) on its side.

Cupping feels good enough to justify its use even if nothing is bothering you.

Cupping with Petroleum Jelly

Rub a thin coating of the jelly onto your partner's back. Press down into the soft tissues of the back with an empty three inch tumbler. When you lift the tumbler very slowly you will see the flesh rise inside it. Experiment by pressing and lifting the tumbler until you know exactly how far you can raise the glass before the skin breaks contact around the rim and the flesh falls back. You want to stop lifting just before this point. The distance varies somewhat depending on the condition of your partner's back but a half an inch is about average.

Lift the cup and slide it around the soft tissues of the back very slowly. If you stay off the spine and the shoulder blades you should be able to continue a single cupping motion around the back for five minutes or more. It's impossible to describe the delicious rolling feeling of the moving cup. Have a friend try it on you.

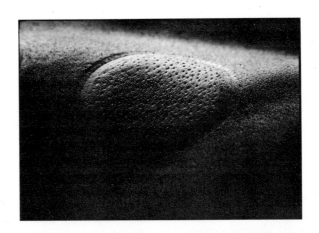

Bamboo Hacking

Unless you've visited rural China where this technique alone is sometimes used as a complete massage treatment, the chances are you've never seen anything like Bamboo Hacking. Using a razor cutter or very sharp thin bladed knife cut six ten inch slits in the end of two three foot-long bamboo rods.

Hold the rods firmly and hack the back lightly with the frayed ends. Stay off the spine but work the entire back and up and down the legs. Once again the back and legs are your instrument. Play them softly like a fine drum. If it sounds right it feels good. 🌿

Group Massage

Here is your chance to find out why the Polynesian kings, the ones with thirty wives, were always smiling. Two (or more—you work it out) people can give a single partner a complete massage. Use several bowls for oil and put them where they can be shared conveniently.

Work on opposite arms, legs, hands, and feet together. Stroke in unison on the long strokes like circulation and draining. On the shorter strokes, the ones that concentrate on a single small part of the body, you don't need to use identical movements. The important thing in group massage is to keep pressures about even. Be silent. Let your hands say it. 🌿

Pregnancy

Like all creative experiences, pregnancy is a great joy and an immense strain. Massage not only eases the strain on a woman's body, it also physically involves her man in the growth of his unborn child. A complete body massage, like the one we have described earlier, works beautifully throughout pregnancy if the masseur observes a few simple precautions. Abdominal strokes are fine in the first three months only. Go easy on these strokes though—no deep kneading or intense pressures. It's best to skip percussion movements and leg pumping because of the extra pressure these strokes can exert on the abdominal area. Be particularly careful when massaging the lower back. Easy pressure here in the first three months works best. After that, work over this area with light, superficial strokes and concentrate on the rest of the body. Oil the breasts and abdomen regularly to prepare the skin for the stretching that will occur as the pregnancy progresses.

If your physician feels that everything is going well, you can begin massage again three days after delivery. Begin by working only on the arms, legs, and head. By the tenth day, or whenever your lady feels comfortable on her side and abdomen, you should be able to start easy stroking on the back, chest, and abdomen. Massage after pregnancy can counteract the general weakness which results from inactivity. It strengthens muscles throughout the body, particularly those of the abdomen and pelvic floor. The intense depression that many women feel after a delivery is not necessarily psychological. Very often its causes can be traced to the overwhelming muscular fatigue that follows birth. Use massage to restore muscle tone and she may be smiling again in a few days. 🌿

Massaging Infants and Children

Babies love to be touched. They love it so much that sometimes they react to a casual squeeze as though it were part of a massage. Don't try to work through an entire massage or even a long sequence of strokes with an infant. Once you start rubbing it won't be long before the baby starts touching back. Sometimes they break up laughing halfway through a stroke. If the baby starts crying while you're pumping a leg that means stop pumping the leg. Use massage to play with a baby and spread good feelings.

Except for an occasional kiss or pat on the back many parents stop touching their kids after the age of five or six. Why not be warm to your child? It helps him feel good about himself and everyone else. Children enjoy massage most at the end of the day when they're tired and slowed down. If your child jumps up in the middle of a stroke let it go. They always come back.

Someday, hopefully, children will learn massage in primary school physical education programs. Such knowledge would certainly temper the training in competitive sports that teach them to overcome each other.

{Erotic Massage}

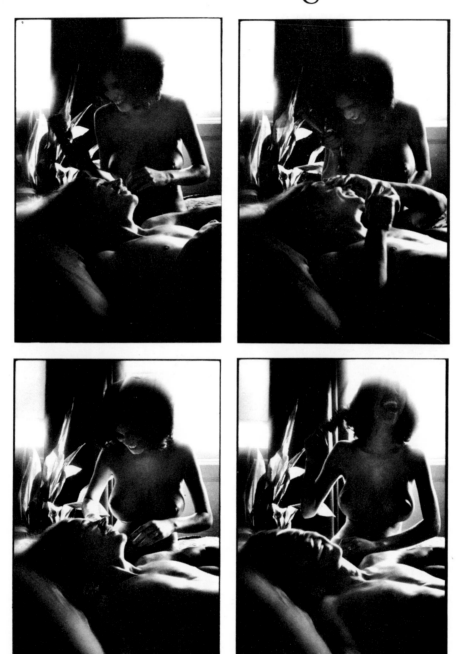

*E*very bookstore has modern sex manuals that are overflowing with advice on 'new sex techniques'. All of us, they claim, can be fantastic lovers, virtuosi in the art of seduction, if only we knew the right way to manipulate the body of the opposite sex. In the grand American tradition, we are given more information on how to operate the machine. First, a complete list of parts. Anatomical ignorance, argues the modern sex manual, is a primary cause of sexual problems. Learn the names and function of all the parts. Great debates rage on over whether this information should be dispensed at home or in school: exactly where should your child learn the names and functions of all the parts? Great lovers, we are led to believe, are experts who know which buttons to press to make seduction, foreplay, and climax occur precisely on schedule.

Despite these lurid promises there is no way on earth you can turn on someone who doesn't care for you. Eroticism is a force that flows *between* two people and it's usually evident and real before you lay hands on each other. It has absolutely nothing to do with parts, labels, or proper technique. This part of the book is for people who feel each other. Lovers. Here are some ways other lovers have touched.

Rub a fine spray of perfumed powder
into your lover's body from head to toe.
no kneading, no hacking, no pounding,
Just fingertips.
    You know how your man feels
    You know how your woman feels
    We want to speak to both of you be-
ginning here . . . 🍂

Touch the inside of his ear, lightly, circle it with one finger slowly. Circle the outside of the ear evenly. Brush into the tiny half moon below his lobe. Have you touched him there before? Later he may touch you the same way . . . ❧

Brush her eyelids. Her eyes remain closed, feeling your hands. Touch her lips. Tiny circles over her smooth cheeks. Stroke the side of her neck with three fingertips . . . ❧

Your hot breath on his neck. Breathe
on him. Brush his inner arm with two
fingertips. Circle his nipples with your
tongue . . . 🦋

Stroke the sides of her breasts in a long figure eight down her sides. Press one finger into her navel. Breathe on her nipples . . . 🍃

Breathe on his stomach. Circle his navel with your tongue—hot breath on naked skin . . . 🍃

Bite her gently on the back of her knee. Stroke the inside of her thighs with your tongue. Press both buttocks. Feel her move . . . 🍃

Your tongue on his spine, up and down . . . again. Stroke the top of his shoulders lightly with two fingers. Brush the sides of his back with your breasts . . . 🍃

Stroke the inside of her thighs with your fingertips. Lift her knees. Stroke her thighs again, once again. Press your fingers between her toes . . . ❧

Feel her breathe under your hands. The pulse in her neck, smooth breasts, her dark hair twisted against your naked arms . . . ❧

Stroke the heel of his hand and the ridge just below the base of his fingers. Touch him lightly, there, with one fingertip . . . ❧

Appendix

4.

{ Accessories }

A Massage Table

If you want to incorporate massage into your life as a daily or weekly pleasure, a massage table is a wonderful thing to have in your home. A table totally relieves the occasional strain of working on the floor and actually makes the experience even more satisfying for your partner. The simple design shown here is strong, and inexpensive. It will outlast your car, T.V. or stereo and give you a great deal more pleasure than all three of them combined.

Be sure to sand all surfaces thoroughly. You may want to varnish or paint the wood since a carefully designed and built massage table is a beautifully functional piece of furniture. Whatever elaborations you add to this basic design, remember you don't want your table to end up looking like a hospital appliance. The finished piece should be warm and inviting. If you have a few extra dollars to spend, cover your mattress with fitted satin sheets.

The table should be long enough to support the entire body. The thirty inch width allows your partner's arms to lie comfortably at his side when he is on his back. When he turns onto his stomach fold both arms so that they hang over the side of the table from the elbow down. Thirty inches supports the arm to the elbow in this position. If you're massaging small children, design your table so that it supports your child's folded arm right up to the elbow joint. Use the shelf for oils, incense, towels, a vibrator, and other accessories. Keep the table in a warm quiet place where you can move around it easily.

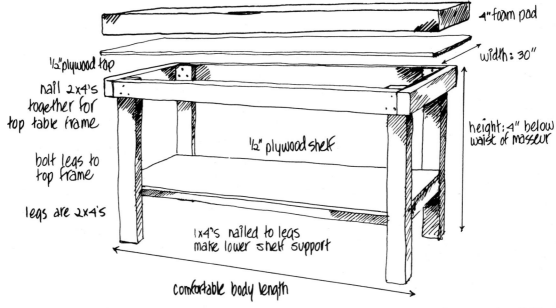

½"plywood top

nail 2x4's together for top table frame

bolt legs to top frame

legs are 2x4's

4" foam pad

width: 30"

½" plywood shelf

height: 4" below waist of masseur

1x4's nailed to legs make lower shelf support

comfortable body length

A Massage Room

Work on a room until it *feels* mellow. The room's design is largely a question of individual taste. Most people enjoy fixtures for candles, incense, and oil lamps. Hang them from the ceiling if you like. A sound source with earphones is a fine touch. Thick rugs and pillows. Soft diffused light during the day. Colored glass in the windows. Plants and flowers. Everything in a massage room should delight the senses.

Once you have set aside a room, or part of a room, as a place for massage you can install infra-red lamps (*not* ultra-violet sun lamps) to warm your partner. A five minute exposure on each side of the body at the beginning and end of a massage spreads a deliciously penetrating warmth throughout the entire body. Very often this simple measure greatly enhances the effects of the massage itself as it relaxes your partner in advance and makes him more receptive to the movements.

Hang three infra-red lamps from a rack over your table. Adjust the height of your lamps so that the three circles of light they produce cover the entire table evenly. Usually a height of two and a half to three feet is about right. With a little extra effort you can make the lamp rack adjustable so it can be raised above your head while you're working and lowered when you want to warm your partner. One way to do this is by attaching the mechanism for raising and lowering an ordinary ceiling lamp to your rack.

If you prefer to keep the lamps at a fixed point above the table, install a dimmer switch in the line to vary the heat intensity. When you turn the switch down the lamps cool, hum a bit, and glow a dull red. There are a few simple precautions to be aware of when you use heat lamps of any kind. Turn them off immediately if, for any reason, your partner becomes uncomfortable. Never use lamps for more than ten minutes on each side of the body and always keep them at least a foot and a half away from the skin. Use heat before and after massage, not while you're working.

There are other additions that make the room comfortable and easy to use. Include an electrical outlet for a vibrator in the center of your lamp rack or very near the table. Be sure to arrange the outlet so that the vibrator cord doesn't drag over your partner. A small waist high table near the massage table is a handy extra platform for oils, incense, and alcohol. The room should be near a sink and a bath or shower. Keep it warm and quiet and far, far away from the distractions of this world. ❧

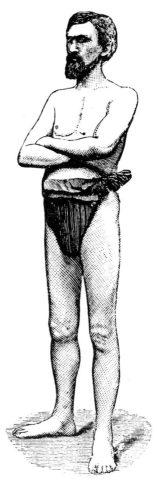

Fig. 41.—From a photograph. Shows the condition of the patient before Dr. Playfair began to treat him with massage.

Fig. 42.—From a photograph. Shows the patient's condition after eight weeks of massage and feeding.

(From "Disorders of Digestion," by Dr. T. Lauder Brunton.)

Graham, op. cit.

Truly, it was to our amazement that the ailing said they were well. Being Europeans, we thought we had given away to doctors and priests our ability to heal. But here it was, still in our possession . . . it was ours after all, we were more than we had thought we were.—*Cabeza de Vaca.*[6]

There are ways that men can heal one another without drugs, without words, and without prayer. It is the physician who has recorded these ways for the past two thousand years while lovers, witchdoctors, and courtesans have practiced them silently. In the earliest records people used massage to bless each other.

'And after she had bathed him and anointed him with olive oil, and cast about him a goodly mantle, he came forth from the bath in fashion like the deathless gods.'—*Homer.*[7]

The exquisite blend of science and humanism that thrived in ancient Greece flourished because everyone had plenty of time. Philosophers devoted lifetimes to the revelations of a single intricately woven dialog. Physicians spent hours working on a patient who complained of sore muscles and joints. Herodicus, one of the masters of Hippocrates in the fifth century BC, used massage to prolong the lives of elderly patients. He was so successful that Plato reproached him for protracting the painful existence of the aged. Despite this criticism he had himself massaged regularly until the day of his death at the age of 104.[8]

Socrates felt that massage was only less necessary to human life than wheat and barley, the grains that kept men alive. Greek healers used massage as a primary healing tool and as a means of assuaging pain. 'The physician must be experienced in many things,' says Hippocrates, 'but assuredly also in rubbing. For rubbing can bind a joint that is too loose and loosen a joint that is too rigid. . . . Rubbing can make flesh and cause parts to waste. Hard rubbing binds, soft rubbing loosens; much rubbing causes parts to waste; moderate rubbing makes them grow.'[9] The movement of the blood was not understood, but Hippocrates emphasized the importance of rubbing toward the heart. Two thousand years later William Harvey demonstrated the principles of blood circulation and immediately lost his practice.

Romans, as you might expect, were crazy for massage. It existed there as a marvelously effective medical technique and as a complement to the courtesan's art. Once again, only therapeutic records have survived. Cicero, the great orator, philosopher, and statesman (BC 106–43) felt that he owed as much of his health to his anointer as he did to his physician. Regular massage helped improve his feeble health and eventually overcome a violent speech defect. The famous advocate, Pliny, never a strong man, was almost destroyed by a severe illness at the height of his career. He was treated by a physician who cured his patients by rubbing their bodies with olive oil. Pliny's health was so dramatically improved by the treatment that he asked the emperor to grant the healer (who, like many physicians in Rome, was either a Jew or a Greek) full Roman citizenship. Julius Caesar had himself massaged daily to relieve headaches and neuralgia.[10]

---

[6]Haniel Long. *Interlinear to Cabeza De Vaca.* Frontier Press. Pittsburgh, Pennsylvania: 1969. p. 11.
[7]Homer. *The Odyssey.* Book I, part iii, line 446.
[8]Graham, op. cit., p. 5.
[9]Ibid., p. 6.
[10]Ibid., p. 9.

Percussion technique enjoyed a separate popularity in Rome. Masseurs used a wooden palette shaped somewhat like a ping-pong racket to restore tone to the muscles all over the body. The effects of these percussion treatments were so impressive that the technique was appropriated by a kind of massage black market. In the large cities there were establishments where Patricians brought ailing, deformed, or elderly slaves for a series of treatments that would temporarily rejuvenate them and increase their market value. These places had rotten reputations but nevertheless women went to them secretly, hoping to restore their youth or their figure . . . 'yielding to their vanity, they endured the blows of the palette, which it was necessary to use at a great rate . . .'[11]

Galen (AD 130–200), the physician who had been described as 'the most accomplished man of his age, whose authority in medical matters was regarded in Europe as almost supreme for a thousand years,' was deeply committed to the use of massage in treating a wide variety of ailments. He warns against the use of sudden violent movements and recommends warming the entire body with the hands before oiling it. Like many other physicians Galen combined massage with exercise to keep his patients fit.[12]

Massage, like everything else the Romans were into, eventually got out of control. The emperor Hadrian found himself passing out oil to prevent soldiers from rubbing themselves against slippery stone columns at the public baths. People started massaging dogs and horses. 'Lift her up by the tail, and having given her a stretching let her go. And she will shake herself when let go, and show that she liked the treatment.' (Arrian, Cynegeticus). Patrician families spent hours lying around the baths being treated by castrated, speechless massage slaves whose only function in life was to rub their masters.[13]

The Greeks and Romans were not the only people who were committed to the use of massage. When Alexander invaded India he found that 'the King while receiving foreign visitors listens and is rubbed at the same time.' Two hundred years before Alexander the Sanskrit Ayur-Veda (Art of Life) suggested that one 'rise early, bathe, wash the mouth, anoint the body, submit to friction and shampoo and then exercise.'[14]

Early experiments with massage in China revealed the direct relationship between skin surface pressures and the health of internal organs. Acupuncture theory developed the specific details of this discovery. The acupuncturist understands these relationships so precisely that by inserting needles about a tenth of an inch into the flesh he can regulate the functions of any part of the body. Acupuncture, of course, is not massage; although on rare occasions it can be painful, it's a therapy that seems to work. Since causing pain is not one of the objects of the treatment we can no more condemn it here than we would surgery.

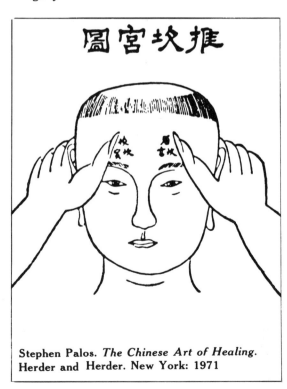

Stephen Palos. *The Chinese Art of Healing.* Herder and Herder. New York: 1971

Massage and acupuncture have grown together in China. Masseurs working with a thorough knowledge of acupuncture points have fantastic reputations as therapists throughout the Orient. Unfortunately, 'folk healing' has been ignored by the Westerners who have controlled China for the past few centuries. As a result, every town and village has its own acupuncturist and, inevitably, opinions differ on correct technique. The Communist government is undertaking a study which will ultimately attempt to systematize China's 4,000 year old folk medicine tradition. Although this immense task is still—after twenty years—only beginning, this much is clear right now: the Chinese are going to give us some dramatic new ways of using massage.

Massage, like sex, seems to be rediscovered periodically. In the year 1593 an Italian botanist named Alpinus brought back the news that no one in Egypt left the bath without being massaged from head to foot. This kind of sensuality was unheard of in Europe where rubbing was something doctors did to part of your body when you were sick. A curious aristocrat who tried the Egyptian version described his experience in these words:

'Perfectly maséed, one feels completely regenerated, a feeling of extreme comfort pervades the whole system, the chest expands, and we breathe with pleasure; the blood circulates with ease, and we have a sensation as if freed from an enormous load; we experience a suppleness and lightness until then unknown. It seems as if we truly lived for the first time. There is a lively feeling of existence which radiates to the extremities of the body, whilst the whole is given over to the most delightful sensations; the mind takes cognizance of these, and enjoys the most agreeable thoughts; the imagination wanders over the universe which it adorns, sees everywhere smiling pictures, everywhere the image of happiness. If life were only a succession of ideas, the rapidity with which memory retraces them, the vigor with which the mind runs over the extended chain of them, would make one believe that in the two hours of delicious calm which follow a great many years have passed.'[15]

Mary, Queen of Scots, contracted a terrible case of typhus in 1566. At the height of the fever everything appeared hopeless, and it looked as though she were going to die. As calmly as possible she struggled through some simple last rites and then all at once her body became cold and rigid. Desperately her attendants bent over the pale form but they could find no pulse or respiration. Everyone gave up any hope for her except her physician, a man by the name of News, who continued to work up and down her body with vigorous massage strokes. After a while she stirred, color returned to her cheeks, and she sat up in bed. From that point on she began to recover despite the fact that her death had already been reported in Edinburgh.[16]

[11]Ibid., p. 11.
[12]Ibid., p. 13.
[13]Ibid., p. 15.
[14]Ibid., p. 17.
[15]Ibid., p. 19.
[16]Ibid., p. 20.

In Ovid's time, when sterile Roman ladies allowed themselves to be whipped with leather straps, nobody pretended they were being massaged. But in 1698 when Paullini offered a massage treatment for libertines that combined whipping, beating, slapping, and severe versions of the common percussion strokes he was taken quite seriously. There is nothing surprising about any of this since there are still 'therapies' masquerading as massage, which torture people. Ladies and gentlemen who are far too civilized to participate in overt flagellation ceremonies allow themselves to be pounded and pulled half to death by sadistic 'therapists.' The justification for such punishment is always the same: it's good for you. Rest assured though, that if the good Dr. News had beaten Mary, Queen of Scots with a leather belt not only would he have lost his head, but within five minutes Mary herself would have been dead as a beet.

Max Bohm. *Massage: Its Principles and Technic.* W. B. Saunders Company. Philadelphia: 1915

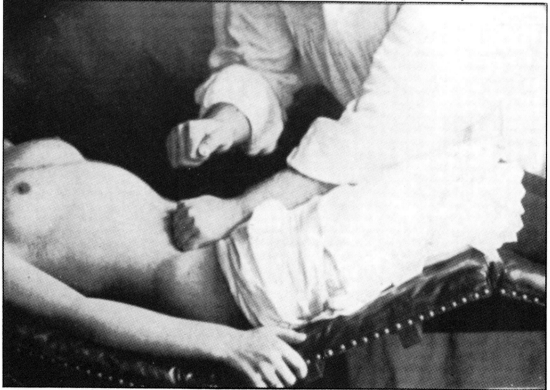

The famous 17th century physician Sydenham was fond of observing that if somebody knew the power of massage and could somehow make this knowledge secret he could make a fortune. Massage has been used daily in every culture, even the most ancient. It would seem as though nothing could be less mysterious; everyone can do it. Yet massage was used to perpetrate one of the most stupendous hoaxes in history.

Eighteenth century France supported an utterly decadent aristocratic class. While the French people starved these nobles cultivated some of the largest lawns the world has ever seen. They dabbled with art, literature, and the occult, and, like aristocrats everywhere, longed for some kind of passionate commitment. Just a few years before the Revolution ended their boredom forever they discovered Anthony Mesmer.

Mesmer's Animal Magnetism sessions seemed to give everyone exactly what they were looking for. If you were ill he cured you and if, as was more often the case, you just wanted a trip, he took off the top of your head.

In the hothouse aristocratic atmosphere of Paris where unbelievable ostentation was the rule, Mesmer's house overwhelmed everyone. Enormous intricately stained glass windows shed a dim religious light on immense rooms which, like Versailles, were lined with mirrors. Antique vases stood on his chimney pieces filled with rare, fabulously expensive incense. Aeolian harps whispered tantalizing melodies from hidden chambers while invisible voices chanted half-heard refrains. 'So wonderful! said the pseudo philosophers, who would believe anything if it were the fashion; So amusing, said the worn out debauchees who had drained the cup of sensuality to its dregs, and who longed to see lovely women in convulsions, with the hope that they might gain some new emotions from the sight.'[17]

Emil A. G. Kleen. *Massage and Medical Gymnastics.* J. & A. Churchill. London: 1918

[17]Charles MacKay, Ll. D. *Extraordinary Popular Delusions and the Madness of Crowds.* Farrar, Straus and Giroux. New York: 1932. Pp. 324–325.

Patients (or trippers) sat around a small tub filled with magnetic water bottles, iron filings, and streaks of colored dye. Once everyone had seen its bizarre contents the tub was covered. The cover itself was surfaced with a number of long iron rods that patients used to press against 'afflicted' parts of the body. Everyone sat in a tight circle holding hands and pressing their bodies together to make it easy for magnetic effects to pass from one person to another.

At this point the assistant magnetizers, usually powerful, handsome young men, entered the room and knelt before the ladies. Treatment began with a firm embrace around the knees. After the embrace each assistant began massaging or 'magnetizing' his lady with his fingertips and hands. At first strokes concentrated on sensitive parts of the body like the neck, spine and other nerve centers. Eventually though, the young man's hands would move directly to the lady's breasts which he would stroke while he fixed her with an intense stare to 'magnetize by the eye.'

While this was going on everything was almost perfectly still. Weird harmonica arpeggios drifted through the room and occasionally a hidden woman's voice sang part of a strange aria. The assistant magnetizers continued the massage while the spectators held their breath. 'Gradually the cheeks of the ladies began to glow, their imaginations to become inflamed; and off they went, one after the other, in convulsive fits. Some of them sobbed and tore their hair, others laughed till the tears ran from their eyes, while others shrieked and screamed and yelled till they became insensible altogether.'

At the absolute crisis of this delirium Mesmer made his entrance, dressed in a long lilac colored silk robe embroidered with gold flowers and waving a white wand. The hidden voices swelled. Once again the eerie sound of wild harmonica notes filled the room. He walked with absolute self assurance and, as his assistants released the frenzied women, Mesmer fixed them with his awesome eyes. He magnetized (massaged) them slowly around the eyes, over the head and back and traced figures on their breasts and abdomen with his magic wand. This stroking brought even the most insensible women back to consciousness and they were immediately confronted with Mesmer's hypnotic gaze. Here, the purely predictable physiological effects of massage gave way once again to hypnotic suggestion. The ladies calmed down. Some swore they felt streams of 'cold or burning vapor' coursing through their bodies when the master touched them.

'It is impossible,' says M. Dupotet, 'to conceive of the sensation which Mesmer's experiments created in Paris. No theological controversy in the earlier ages of the Catholic Church, was ever conducted with greater bitterness.' Admirerers described the treatment with reverence usually reserved for works of God. Others claimed Mesmer was an imposter, a madman, and 'in league with the devil.' The whole city was flooded with pamphlets attacking and defending the doctrine, and in court Marie Antoinette declared herself in favor of it. The uproar went on for several years until a group of level-headed French doctors finally exposed Mesmer and ruined his reputation. The master, in turn, rejected France and left the country with three hundred and forty thousand francs.[18]

[18]Idem.

The persistent hope that man will somehow learn from his follies is mocked by the continuing popularity of quacks who build some kind of practice by exploiting the simple techniques of massage. A hundred years after Mesmer's death the great American physician-masseur Douglas Graham warned that 'in every city of the United States, and indeed, of the whole civilized world, there may be found individuals claiming mysterious and magical powers of curing disease, setting bones, and relieving pain by the immediate application of their hands. Some of these boldly assert that their art, or want of art is a gift from Heaven, due to some unknown power which they call magnetism, while others designate it by some peculiar word ending with pathy or cure, and it is often astonishing how much credit they get for their supposed genius from many of the most learned people.'[19]

In the beginning of the 19th century, Peter Henrik Ling developed a massage theory which synthesized Greek, Chinese, Egyptian and Roman techniques. Ling's methods were spread from his native Sweden by disciples and became immensely popular throughout Europe. Physicians all over the world looked to Swedish medical schools for comprehensive information on massage. The term 'Swedish Massage' does not refer to a specific method; it merely acknowledges the fact that Swedish schools continue to functions as centers for therapeutic massage techniques. Masseurs trained in these schools do not limit themselves to a single approach.[20]

Max Bohm. *Massage: Its Principles and Technic*, op. cit.

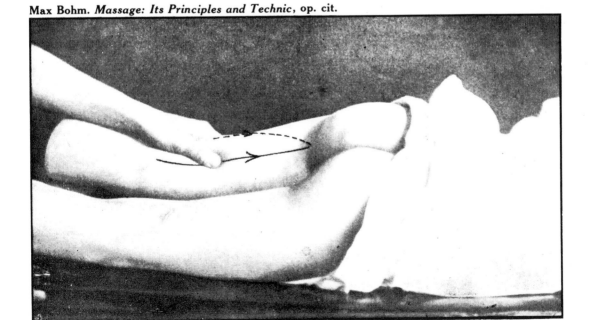

[19]Graham, op. cit., p. 21.
[20]Hartvig Nissen. *Practical Massage and Corrective Exercises*. F. A. Davis Company. London: 1916. p. 5.

Towards the middle of the nineteenth century, in the opening years of the industrial era, men took up what has become a modern obsession: the worship of machines. Manual labor of any kind came to be looked down upon and doctors started losing interest in massage. People were discovering machines to do everything else—why not a massage machine? Several designs were tried—fortunately none of them have survived. 🍃

Emil A. G. Kleen. *Massage and Medical Gymnastics*, op. cit.

C5

D3

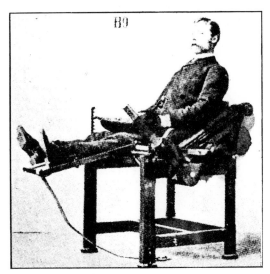

B9

The sexually repressive Victorian period (combined with a pervasive puritan influence in America) made it very difficult for people to touch each other for any reason. A number of fine massage books were published around the turn of the century but the writers found themselves in an unusually difficult position. They had before them the accumulated massage lore of the centuries. And all through history the same theme was repeated: massage is a sensual art. It heals because it feels so good. Victorian therapists, however, would not recognize pleasure as a healing principle. Masseurs, like surgeons, were expected to be cold and impersonal. In keeping with the strictures of the time, writers scrupulously ignored the sensual aspects of massage. These books were careful to emphasize the undeniable fact that nobody was getting off on the treatment.

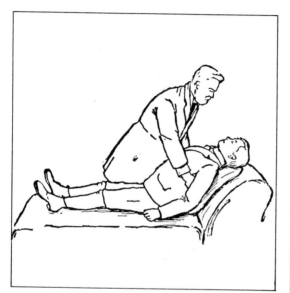

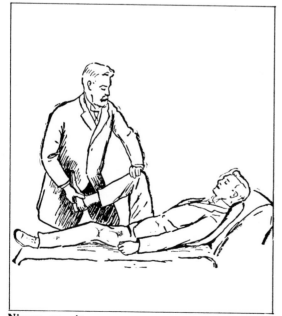

Nissen, op. cit.

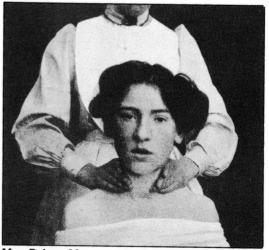

Max Bohm. *Massage: Its Principles and Technic,* op. cit.

The same pressures reinforced by rigid censorship laws forced photographers to present massage as a grotesque ordeal. One French text offers page after page of abdominal technique. The men being massaged all have their pants on, flys coyly open just far enough so as not to offend anybody. The positioning of the hands is correct but a suit and tie make as much sense on a massage table as skis do in a bathtub.

M. Bourcart. *Le Ventre Etude Anatomique et Clinique de la Cavite Abdominale au point de vue du Massage.* Paris: 1904.

Common sense as well as four thousand years of medical records indicates that massage works best when it is a sensual experience. Victorians ignored this evidence and those few who were still dedicated to the use of massage strived to make it scientific and thus acceptable to their age. Massage specialists spent years in dusty libraries pouring over gigantic treatises on anatomy and physiology to learn the 'correct' way of touching other people. Massage, like psychology, was transformed from a common folk healing technique to a science whose secrets were supposedly only available to the initiated. The intensive research efforts of this group did give us a great deal of important information about the specific effects of massage on various diseases. But their conclusions regarding technique are usually nothing more than the translation of ancient massage methods into a modern idiom, the language of science.

Dr. J. B. Zabludowski, Professor of Massage.

Every so often one of these specialists made contact with an isolated tribe somewhere in the world where, quite mysteriously, almost everyone had mastered massage. Victorians forced massage into clinics where it was associated with sickness and suffering. Outside their unhappy world it continued to function as a sensual art and a delightful form of play. Here, once again, sensual massage is 'discovered' by a European, this time in the Sandwich Islands:

'Wherever you stop for lunch or for the night, if there are native people near, you will be greatly refreshed by the application of *lomi-lomi* . . . To be *lomi-lomied* you lie down upon a mat and undress for the night. The less clothing you have on, the more perfectly the operation can be performed. To you thereupon comes a stout native with soft, fleshy hands, but a strong grip, who, beginning with your head and working down slowly over the whole body, seizes and squeezes with a quite peculiar art every tired muscle, working and kneading with indefatigable patience, until in half an hour, whereas you were weary and worn out, you will find yourself fresh, all soreness and weariness absolutely and entirely gone, and mind and body soothed to a healthful and refreshing sleep. The *lomi-lomi* is used not only by the natives, but among almost all the foreign residents and not merely to procure relief from weariness consequent on over-exertion, but to cure headaches, to relieve the aching of neuralgic and rheumatic pains, and by the luxurious as one of the pleasures of life.'[21]

Despite 'discoveries' like this one the aversion to massage as a gross physical act has carried over to the present. Contemporary doctors will go to great lengths to avoid laying a hand on a patient. It's easier and faster to prescribe pain killers that dull the entire nervous system than to massage the head and neck to cure a headache. Very often modern therapists avoid massage simply because they don't have the time or the inclination to be that good to other peo-

[21]Graham, op. cit., p. 33.

ple. When they do use it too often the 'patient' is treated in dungeon-like rooms where he is manipulated mechanically without a trace of compassion. That kind of massage feels exactly the way it looks.

Most modern hospitals are so ugly and impersonal that it would seem that the patients are being punished for being sick. Perhaps someday there will be a room in each hospital full of beauty. A place where, for an hour or so, men and women can forget about chromium appliances, white walls, drugs, and suffering. A room of wood, incense, flowers and music—a place for massage and pleasure.

Right now you have all you need. You can be a healer, a courtesan, a magician, a lover.

You can be warm. 🌿

Friends
of Massage:
Gretchen Schields
set design, illustrations
and scapegoat; Lee Wakefield,
psychological counseling, dinner;
Robert and Barbara Freeman—reality;
the people in the photographs are real, not
professional models—as you can see they enjoyed
each other: Bob Dragge, Steve Eagle,
Kristine Feline, Lory Gilkerson, Elijah Hudspeth,
Gordon Inkeles, Little & Buck, Mishugina, Kate Maycox
and Pooh Bear, Timothy Motzko, Suzanne
Paisley, Bud Pragerson, Christina Sanchez, Robert Scheu,
Anne Skillion, Virginia, Lori Toppi, and Joanna Sweig.
Thank you Melody Rogers, Sandra Scott, John Grissim,
Stevie Lipney, and Manuel Azevedo.

Production: Barbara Kelman and Dian-Aziza Oóka.
Massagee: Alan Rinzler.

Also in Unwin Paperbacks

DO-IT-YOURSELF SHIATSU
Wataru Ohashi

Shiatsu, the ancient Japanese art of acupressure, combines some of the best features of acupuncture, massage, yoga-like exercises and oriental medicine. The fact that no needles are involved means that you can practise Shiatsu both on other people and yourself.

Literally Shiatsu means finger pressure. It uses the same tsubo or pressure points as acupuncture and relies on the same channels of energy throughout the body. Like acupuncture, when skilfully performed Shiatsu can relieve pain and tension – complaints as varied as arthritis, headaches, haemorrhoids, menstrual cramps, impotence and frigidity have all been treated successfully with it – and it teaches you to avoid ailments such as indigestion, nervous tension and heart disease by cultivating a balanced diet and way of life. What is more, Shiatsu is enjoyable as well as effective.

Included in the book are some 150 photographs and diagrams demonstrating exercises, massage and techniques for treating every part of the body. There are also charts showing you where the tsubo and Yin and Yang meridian lines are situated and an excellent introduction explaining the origins of Shiatsu and the difference between Eastern and Western attitudes towards medicine and the body.

THE ACUPRESSURE SLIMMING BOOK
Dr Frank Bahr

Dr Frank Bahr, one of Europe's leading medically qualified acupressure experts, sets out a safe and simple way to conquer the urge to overeat – the heart of any diet problem. Every year thousands of people lose weight through dieting but are disappointed because they quickly put on weight again.

Dr Bahr has discovered the pressure points on the body that control appetite, the significance of which was not appreciated by the ancient Chinese who practised acupressure (a form of gentle massage of selected points on the body – acupuncture without needles).

The Acupressure Slimming Book shows you how to do daily acupressure exercises, *which are easy to perform and can be done at home or at work*. These 10 second exercises curb the urge to overeat – and so enable you both to lose weight successfully and, once you have lost weight, not to put it back on.

Also provided are diets used and tested in Dr Bahr's own health clinic (since if you eat less, *what* you eat becomes extremely important), with menus that are tasty and varied enough to make sure you don't suffer from lack of protein or vitamins. In addition, he gives useful hints on how to keep fit, puts forward some intriguing theories as to why people overeat and explains in detail exactly how the acu-diet method works. In Dr Bahr's own words 'diet combined with acupressure unfailingly leads to lasting success'.